studio **7.5**

# Digital Colour

for the **Internet** and other **Media**

| 1 | 2 | 3 | 4 | 5 | 6 | 7 | 8 | 9 |

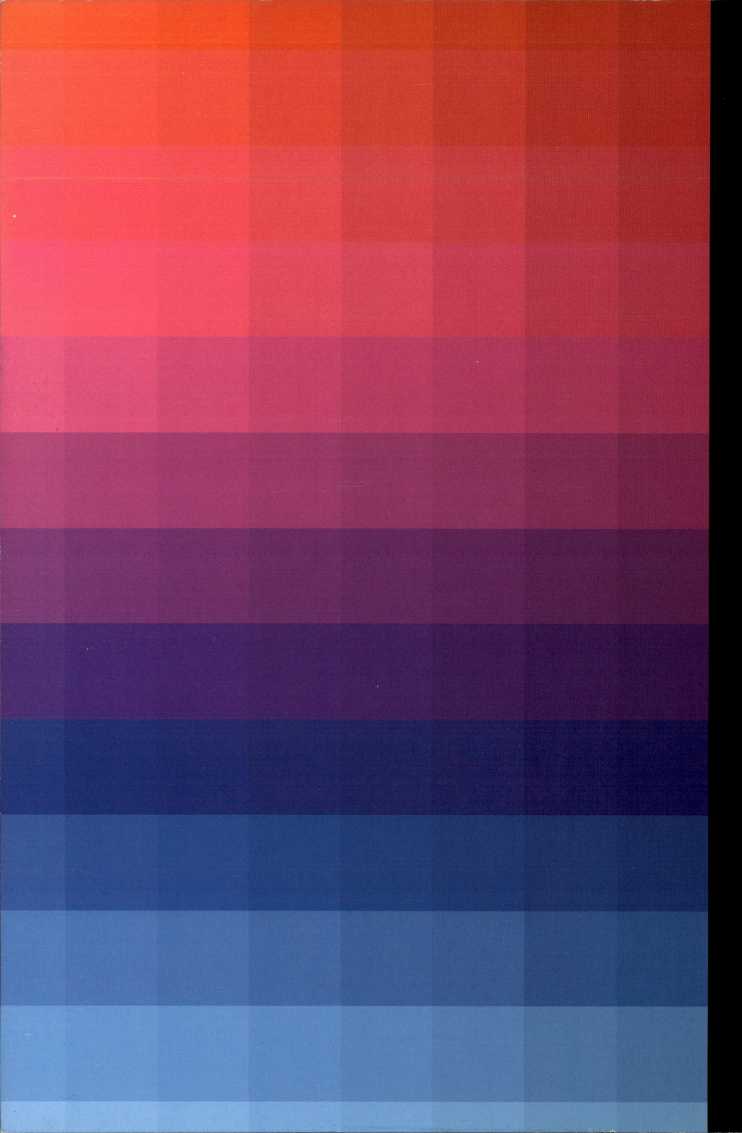

Published by AVA Publishing SA
rue du Bugnon 7
CH-1299 Crans-près-Céligny
Switzerland
Tel: +41 786 005 109
Email: enquiries@avabooks.ch

Distributed by Thames and Hudson (ex-North America)
181a High Holborn
London WC1V 7QX
United Kingdom
Tel: +44 20 7845 5000
Fax: +44 20 7845 5055
Email: sales@thameshudson.co.uk
www.thameshudson.com

Distributed by Sterling Publishing Co., Inc.
in USA
387 Park Avenue South
New York, NY 10016-8810
Tel: +1 212 532 7160
Fax: +1 212 213 2495
www.sterlingpub.com

in Canada
Sterling Publishing
c/o Canadian Manda Group
One Atlantic Avenue, Suite 105
Toronto, Ontario M6K 3E7

English Language Support Office
AVA Publishing (UK) Ltd.
Tel: +44 1903 204 455
Email: enquiries@avabooks.co.uk

ISBN 2-88479-026-8

10 9 8 7 6 5 4 3 2 1

Design by Studio 7.5, Berlin
Photographs by Susanne Stage
English translation by David Wilby, Berlin

Production and separations by AVA Book Production Pte. Ltd., Singapore
Tel: +65 6334 8173
Fax: +65 6334 0752
Email: production@avabooks.com.sg

AVA Publishing SA
Switzerland

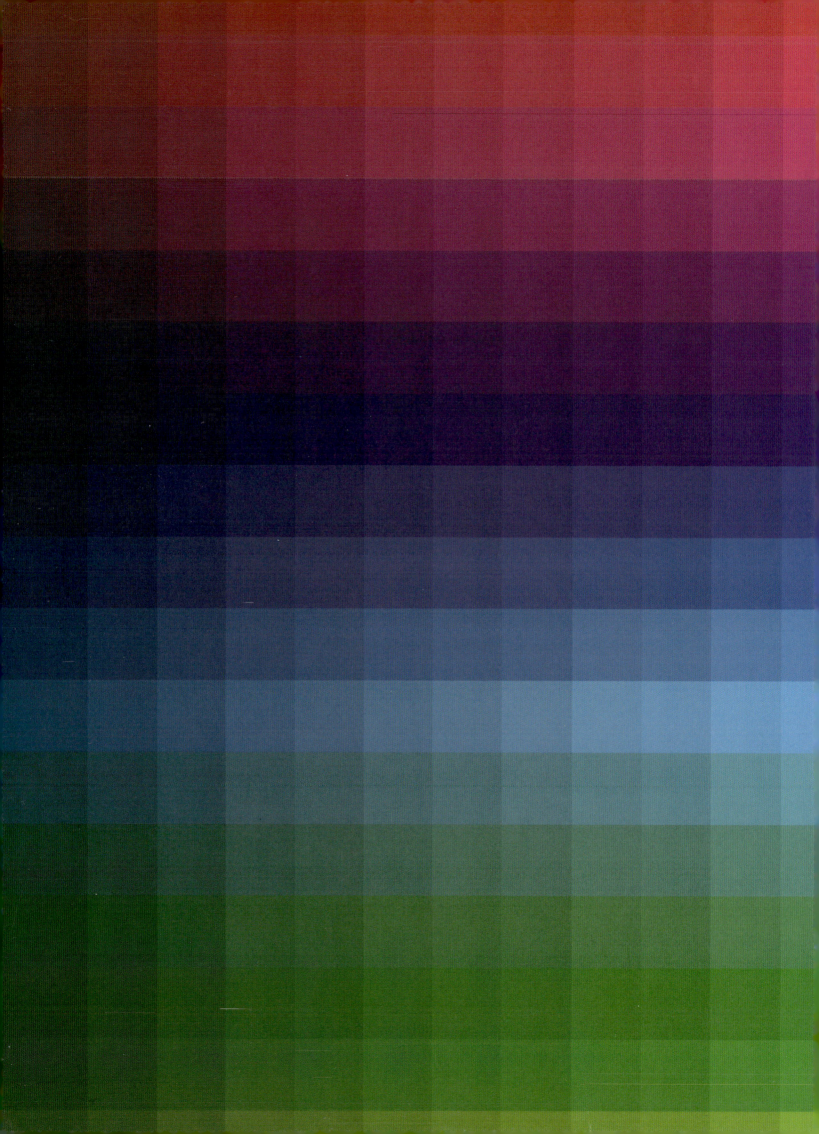

studio **7.5**

# Digital Colour
for the **Internet** and other **Media**

| 1 | 2 | 3 | 4 | 5 | 6 | 7 | 8 | 9 |

62|73

**: The Media of Colour**
The media of colour is about the difference between paper and screen. How to be as colour consistent as possible across different media and how important is colour management. We also look at the creative interplay of the two media, paper and screen.

**5**

46|61

**: The Computing of Colour**
This chapter covers screen-based output systems and related terms like colour depth, Web-safe colours and the hexadecimal system. What you need to know about gamma correction and why colours look different on different operating systems.

**4**

# Content

32|45

**: The Order of Colour**
This is a chapter about colour systems. What are the principles to order and naming colours? We explain terms like colour family, tones, tints and shades. We demystify the good old "shoe sole" and finally focus on the relationship of colour and space.

**3**

20|31

**: As we may see**
Here we focus on the human perception. We explain how the eye works, take a look at colour memory, metameric colours and colour temperature. We look behind the tricks of visual illusions and explain why nobody sees in quite the same way.

**2**

12|19

**: There is no Colour only Light**
This chapter explains the physical phenomenon of colour, starting with an introduction to the spectrum and the richness of colour in the physical world.

**1**

**118|145**

**: The Meaning of Colour**

The meaning of colour is based on local traditions. Culture-specific colour connotations are to be taken into consideration by the designer. We provide an overview of the impact of colour traditions on global communication.

**8**

**146|153**

**: Dynamic Colour**

Will the medium change the perception of colour? Time-based colour change and user interaction are discussed in this chapter.

**9**

**104|117**

**: The Ergonomics of Colour**

This chapter shows the importance of colour for usability: the readability of type or the orientation while navigating a website depends on conscious colour design. The use of colour for mapping information and structuring information architecture is a key factor to good Web design.

**7**

**1** **2** **3** **4** **5** **6** **7** **8** **9**

**74|103**

**: The Grammar of Colour**

Here we open the colour toolbox. The eight types of colour contrast and their relevance on the screen are explained with various real-life applications. We complete the chapter with a look at textures, patterns, colour gradients, colour in photography and transparent colours.

**6**

# Introduction

Colour is an integral part of design. Whether working with three-dimensional objects, printed matter or with websites, the designer has to choose a colour. With tangible objects, this choice is often predetermined – some materials are inherently coloured.

A black screen, on the other hand, is like a blank sheet of paper and as the designer you are free to choose without having to consider a budget. Decisions on colour use are left entirely up to you.

This book is a compilation, equipping the designer with the skills needed for implementing colour in a relevant and sophisticated way across a range of digital media. By beginning with an investigation into the basics of human colour perception, this book provides an insight into the way a user ticks. It clarifies the structure of colour systems and explains how they are represented by a computer.

This book takes a detailed look at the technical foundations underlying the digital medium, the specifics of colour on screen and how consistency

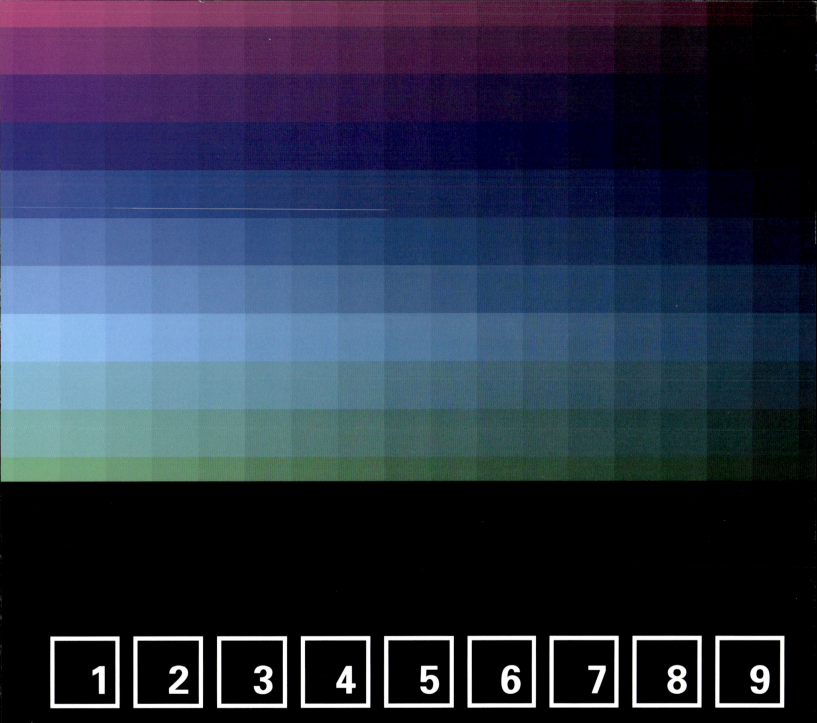

Using examples, ideas for manipulating colour are clearly presented and the factors affecting comfort and readability are explained. In addition, colour is considered as a navigational, sorting, warning and focusing device.

The book provides an overview of the global, regional and local use of colour. The various meanings and

With digital media, colour comes at no extra cost, which prompts the following key questions:
What can be done on the screen that cannot be done on paper? How does the dimension of time and the factor of interaction influence the use of colours?

## How to get the most out of this book

A book about colour on screen represents quite a conceptual challenge. Exactly why this is so will become clear as this book attempts to outline the differences between printed and screen-based forms of media. Certain phenomena typical of the screen are not easily reproduced on paper. Where this is the case, we have used close-ups or exaggerated the effect for purposes of clarity.

Nevertheless, books do present scope for simultaneous comparisons and overviews and, what's more, a fineness of quality (so far) unavailable on the screen.

The phenomenon of colour spans several subject areas that would normally be dealt with by individual books. This book attempts to approach colour as a cross-section running through the classical disciplines. In doing so, the information, clearly divided into **nine chapters**, covers the fundamental physical aspects of light, the physiological particulars of human perception and the technical framework of the screen-based medium itself. Consideration is given to all these areas while retaining the focus on arrangement, effect and the meaning of colour.

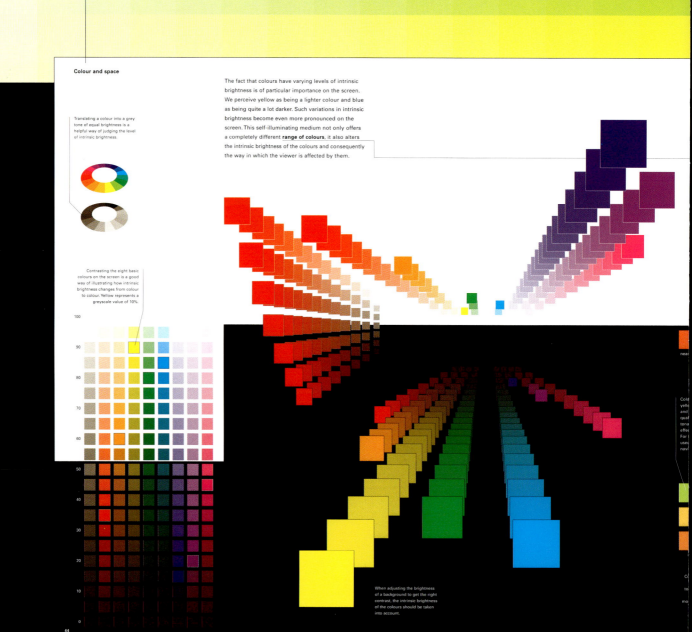

**Colour and space**

The fact that colours have varying levels of intrinsic brightness is of particular importance on the screen. We perceive yellow as being a lighter colour and blue as being quite a lot darker. Such variations in intrinsic brightness become even more pronounced on the screen. This self-illuminating medium not only offers a completely different **range of colours**, it also alters the intrinsic brightness of the colours and consequently the way in which the viewer is affected by them.

Translating a colour into a grey tone of equal brightness is a helpful way of judging the level of intrinsic brightness.

Contrasting the eight basic colours on the screen is a good way of illustrating how intrinsic brightness changes from colour to colour. Yellow represents a greyscale value of 10%.

When adjusting the brightness of a background to get the right contrast, the intrinsic brightness of the colours should be taken into account.

Interconnected themes are accounted for by way of a **hyperlink system** on the pages, that allows the user to find his or her way around the text more easily.

We have taken care not to go into unnecessary detail on a subject, but rather to provide only the information essential to its clarification and understanding. In this way, we aim to make learning a simple and enjoyable process. Perhaps the tips given here will help rationalise a previously found knack for making decisions on colour and back up future choices.

A note on the reading habits of designers: Not only does this book try, in its use of a hyperlink-style reference system, to incorporate the changing nature of reading brought about by the Web, it also corresponds to a visually dominated perception of communication.

Text and pictorial representation are shown as parallel information. Indeed, used purely as a picture book the contents will still make sense.
This reading concept is supported by the modular format of the contents: **One double page – one idea**. Reading can thus begin at any point on the page and proceed in the chosen direction.

The Order of Colour    1  2  **3**  4  5  6  7  8  9

"I will concentrate on the beauty of one blue hill in the distance, and for me, that moment will be eternity."
Alice Walker

see also pages 48|49

Colour effects seen in the world around us are affected by a third dimension – space. The atmosphere, for example, causes the horizon to **appear blue**. Conversely, perceptual experience of this nature affects the way in which we see colours and also how we interpret them and their spatial aspect. Our perception tells us that warmer colours are nearer than colder ones and that saturated colours are nearer than unsaturated ones.

These preconceived attitudes can be used in the design stage to create subconscious effects and to relay information in a way that comes across as plausible.

distant

ment of w-orange her the htness and e therefore en. are widely nphasis and

cold

warm

The light-dark contrast

uced level of ituated more areas of the

Consideration has even been given to the tendency for designers to be a bit impatient: there is no cumbersome **glossary**; terms are clarified as and when they appear in the form of footnotes.

There is no Colour only Light

Colour is first and foremost a physical phenomenon.
This chapter answers the questions "what is light?"
and "what is colour?".
The following overview of fundamental physical
science is the basis for a solid understanding of the
phenomenon of colour. The same principles
also underpin the technology used for screen-based
media of output.

**Light is an electromagnetic wave**

In terms of physics, light consists of electromagnetic waves of varying wavelengths. Of these, only a very small number are **visible** to the human eye and these fall between 380 and 780 **nanometres**.

A mixture of roughly equal amounts of these wavelengths results in white and can be compared to daylight. All other impressions of colour arise through the various possible ways these visible waves can be mixed.

1 nanometre (nm) = $10^{-9}$ metre = 0,000000001 metre = 1 billionth of a metre

| | |
|---|---|
| 100.000.000.000.000 | electricity |
| 10.000.000.000.000 | |
| 1.000.000.000.000 =1km | radio waves |
| 100.000.000.000 | |
| 10.000.000.000 | |
| 1.000.000.000 =1m | |
| 100.000.000 | microwaves |
| 10.000.000 =1cm | |
| 1.000.000 =1mm | |
| 100.000 | infrared |
| 10.000 | |
| 1.000 | |
| 100 | UV |
| 10 | |
| 1 | X-rays |
| 0,1 | |
| 0,01 | gamma radiation |
| 0,001 | |
| 0,000.1 | |
| 0,000.01 | |
| 0,000.001 | |
| 0,000.000.1 | cosmic radiation |

780nm — red, orange, yellow, green, blue, violet — 380nm

The electromagnetic waves are represented on and processed by the **eye's** receptors. Only in the brain does the impression of colour actually form.

see also pages 22|23

"What are these particles? Are they atoms, or molecules, or matter in a still finer state of subdivision?"

J.J. Thomson

Television and other **screen-based media** work using light-generated colours: three wavelengths of light – red, green and blue – are mixed to give a complete range of colours.

see also pages 50|51

The question "what is light?" remains one of science's mysteries. Some phenomena can only be explained if light is a wave...

...other phenomena can only be explained if light is a particle, i.e. the fact that light can be bent by a magnetic field – one property put to use by the cathode-ray tube of the screen.

**Things don't actually have any colour of their own**

Once again, it is light that causes the effect of colour. The so-called **physical colours** of an object only exist in so far that the rebounding light has been altered by the material. Parts of the light spectrum are absorbed by the object and transformed into heat, other parts are reflected.

Take, for example, a "green" leaf – it **absorbs** all waves perceptible to the eye other than those around the 500 nanometre mark. Waves of this length get **reflected**.

If all the light hitting a surface gets absorbed, e.g. the light is completely "swallowed up", the resulting impression of colour is black.

The colour red arises when all wavelengths are absorbed and only red waves are reflected.

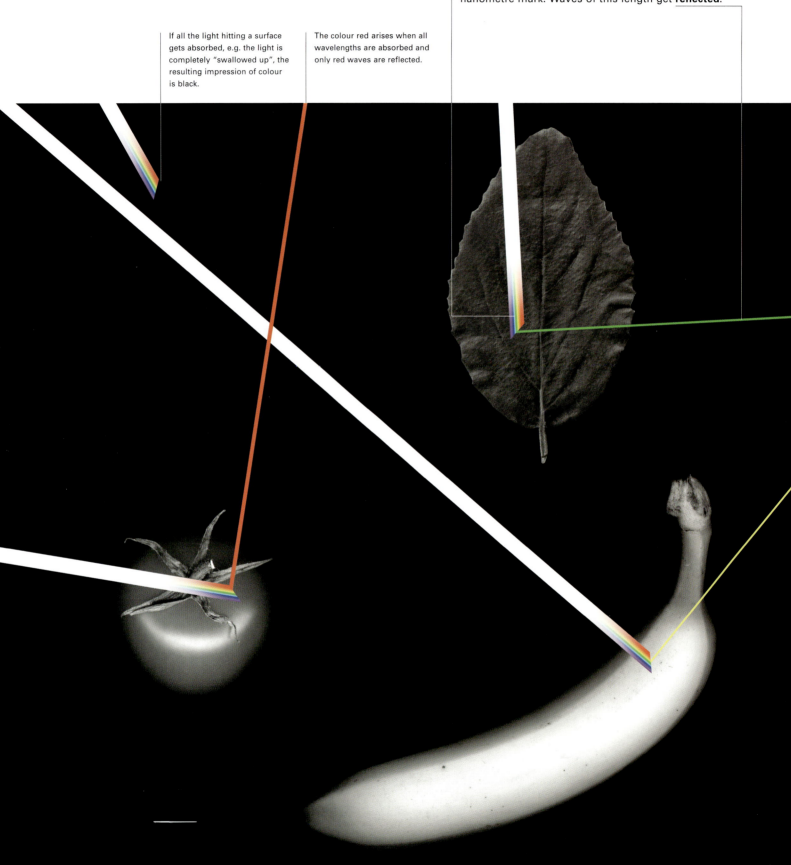

The reflected waves hit the eye's retina. Receptors in
the retina inform the brain of the sensation of light.
The onlooker **perceives** the colour green.

see also pages 22|23

"Colour helps to express light,
not the physical phenomenon,
but the only light that really exists,
that in the artist's brain."

Henri Matisse

Achromatic colours are created
when the complete spectrum is
sent back but at a reduced
Intensity.

The colour yellow arises when
"yellow" waves are reflected, or
indeed if "red" and "green"
waves are reflected in equal
proportions.

"More light!"
Goethe's last words

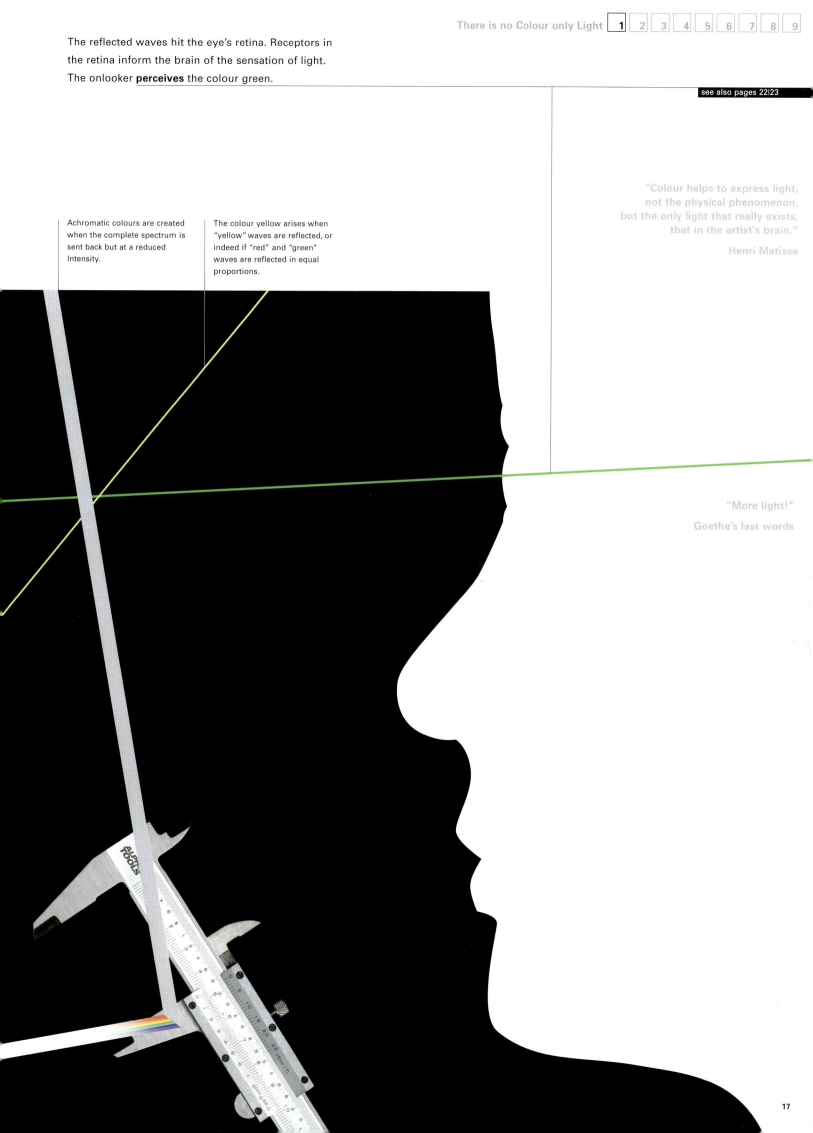

## The richness in colour of the physical world

A material's properties and plasticity influence the way in which the oncoming light is altered, thus determining the surface colour of the object. To be precise, it is possible to separate the various factors affecting the way light is altered: a differentiation may be made between absorption and transmission, as well as between reflection and remission.

**Absorption** means that the waves are swallowed up by the material and transformed into warmth. This makes the object darker.

When parts of the spectrum penetrate the object it is described as **transmission**. If the waves are not diverted, the object will appear transparent, if diverted, the object will appear translucent.

Some surfaces display a prism-like quality, scattering light so that it breaks down into the colours of the spectrum, producing a rainbow effect.

**Remission**
Many materials return light, the resulting effect is a rich, yet matt impression of colour.

**Reflection**
A very smooth surface causes a parallel reflection of the complete spectrum and a mirror-effect results.

**Absorption**
The waves are swallowed up by the material and transformed into warmth which makes the object darker.

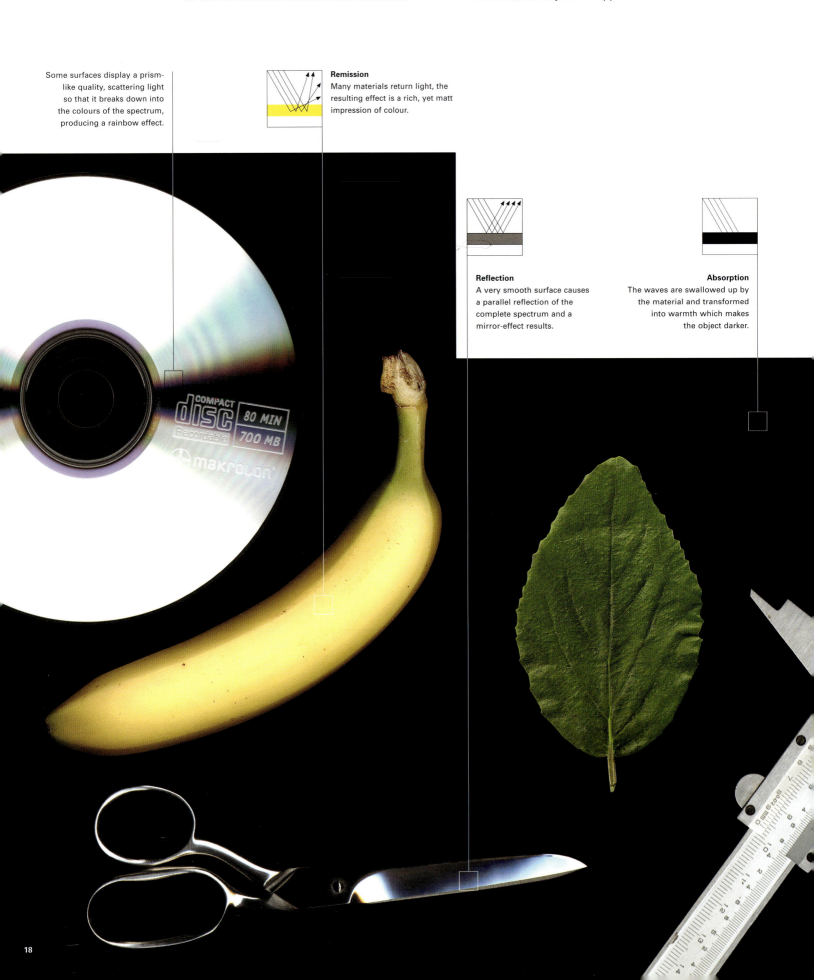

We talk about **remission** if the waves penetrate the outer surface of the material, get diverted and bounce back out again. **Reflection** is caused by light being thrown back directly by the outer surface.

The various ways in which light is altered help us to interpret our surroundings: **modulation in shade** relays data to the eye about an object's third dimension together with its tactile properties and in so doing supports our ability to recognise things.

Photographs, illustrations and **renderings** utilise these factors. Particularly with rendered computer images, the quality of the underlying model representing the physics of light determines the colours and hence the appearance of the image.

see also pages 98|99

**Transmission**
Transparent objects are made of material that has a crystalline structure of such regularity that a greater percentage of light can be transmitted.

**Reflection**
A surface that causes the complete spectrum to be reflected, while at the same time diffusing it, gives off a matt, metallic gleam.

Reflex points, i.e. areas where white light is reflected, provide information as to the curvature and smoothness of an object.

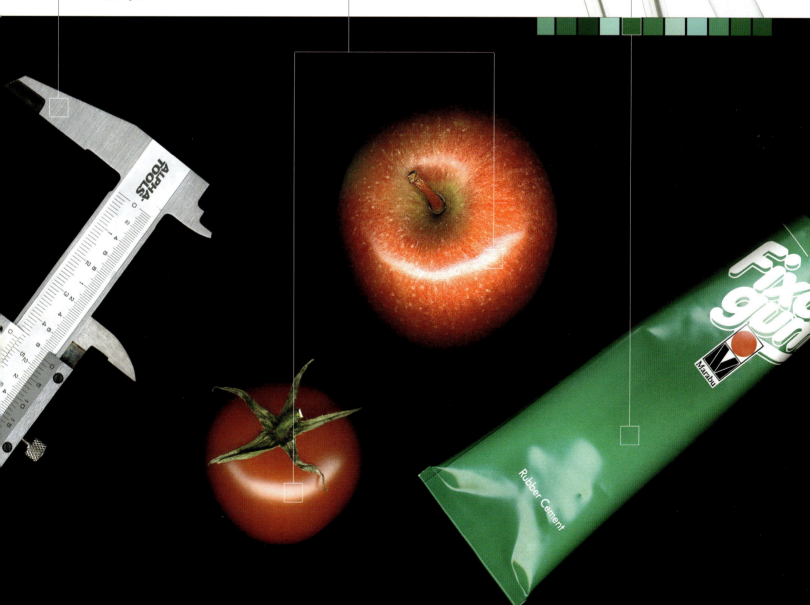

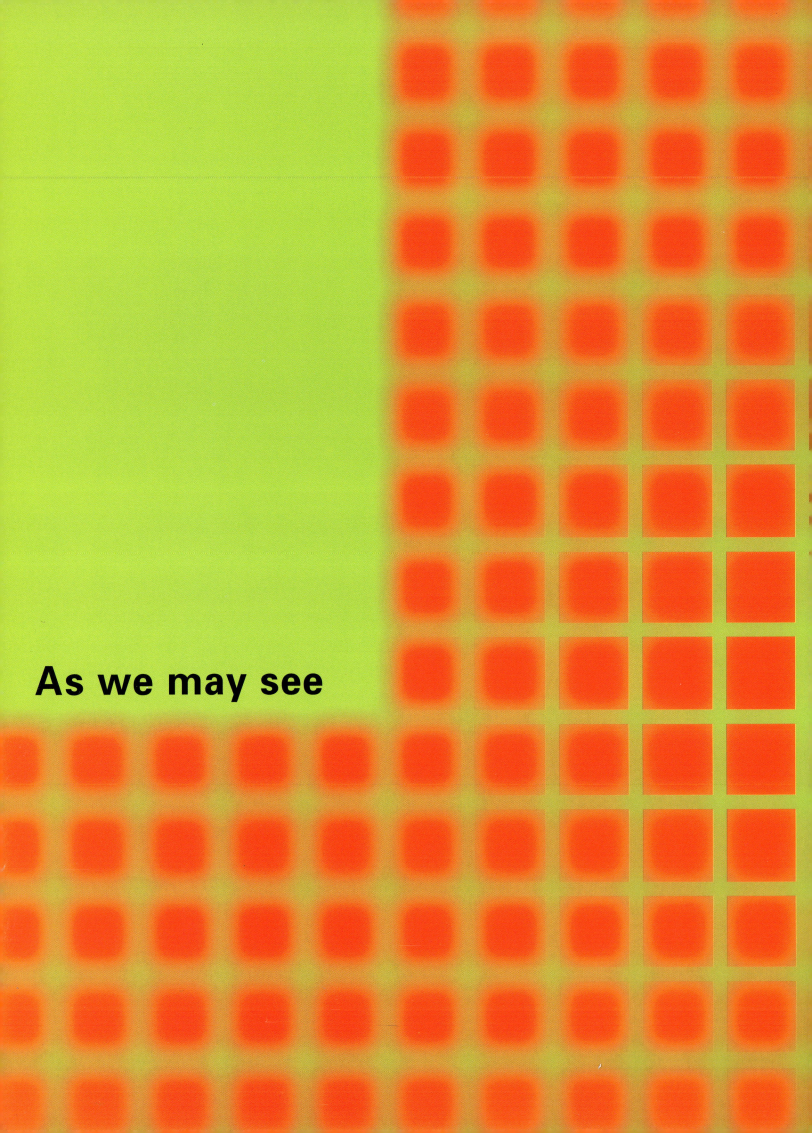

As we may see

1 **2** 3 4 5 6 7 8 9

Colour is also a physiological phenomenon. While
people have long been aware of how the human
eye functions, relatively little research has been done
into how signals are then processed by the perceptive
apparatus.
This chapter outlines the characteristics of human
perception that play a role in the design process.

Light signals entering the eye are bundled by the lens and projected on to the retina. The retina is equipped with two different types of receptors known as rods and cones. These receptors register the intensity and the wavelengths of the light waves hitting them and secrete a substance which acts as a message, relaying the sensation to the perceptive apparatus.

**Rods** are responsible for picking up light-dark variations and probably are also used for adaptation to brightness as well as **simultaneous contrast**.

There are three different varieties of **cone**, corresponding in sensitivity roughly to the three wavelength areas of red, green and blue.

"The only merit I have is to have painted directly from nature with the aim of conveying my impressions in front of the most fugitive effects."
Claude Monet

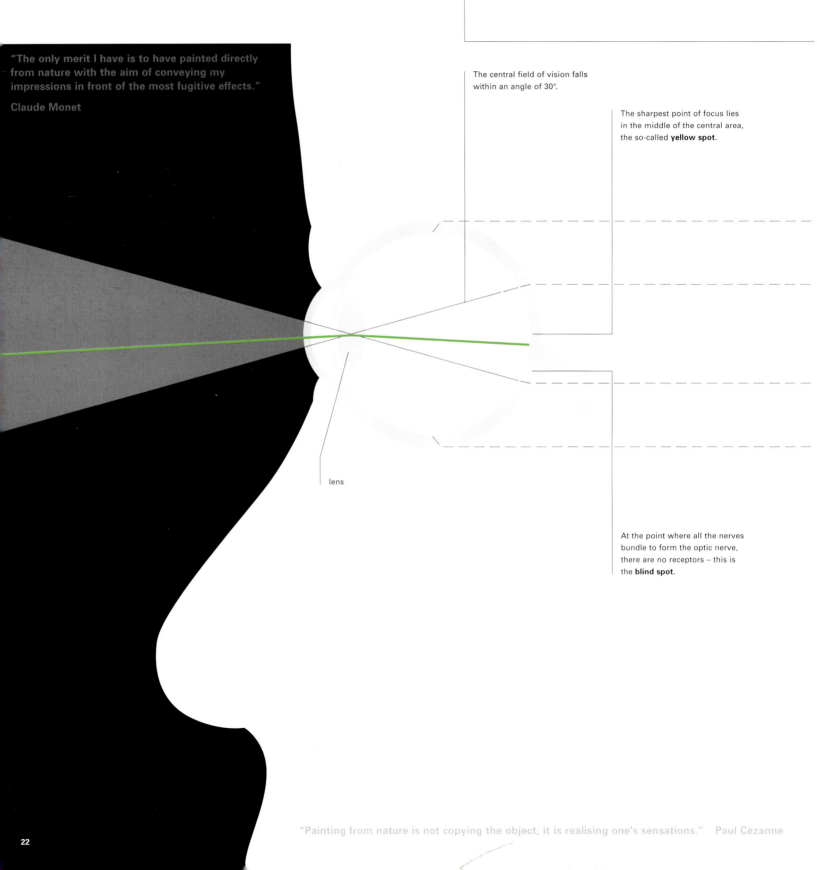

The central field of vision falls within an angle of 30°.

The sharpest point of focus lies in the middle of the central area, the so-called **yellow spot**.

lens

At the point where all the nerves bundle to form the optic nerve, there are no receptors – this is the **blind spot**.

"Painting from nature is not copying the object, it is realising one's sensations."    Paul Cezanne

see also pages 78|79

Interestingly, recent studies suggest that, in contrast
to previous assumptions, our perception is much
more powerful than simple interpretative work and
pattern recognition.
Even with severe impairment to the optical apparatus,
our **perceptive apparatus** is still able to piece together
some kind of sense from the received data.

The distribution of the three
different types of cone on
the retina is shown here as
a percentage.

"There are two things in the painter, the eye and the mind;
each of them should aid the other."

Paul Cézanne

**Cones** are significantly bigger
than rods. In the central field of
vision, there are only "red"
and "green" cones, these are
supplemented by "blue" cones
in the peripheral field of vison.

day

night

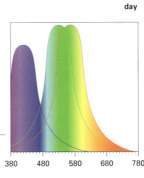

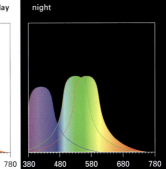

Each cone is **sensitive** to an
area greater than that of the
wavelength covered by just one
colour, which means "green"
cones for example register
wavelengths across a spectrum
of 430–690 nanometres. Green-
yellow represents the area of
greatest sensitivity, that of
around 530 nanometres. This
area is also registered by the
"red" cones, for which the
maximum level of sensitivity
is around 580 nanometres.

**Rods** are somewhat smaller than
cones. The central field of vision
comprises comparatively few rods,
with the distribution increasing
for the peripheral field of vision.

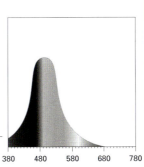

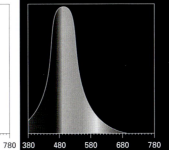

Rods are **sensitive** to an area of
between 380–630 nanometres,
meaning that they comprise the
shorter wave receptors. Because
rods are more sensitive than
cones, they are the ones we use
most at night, hence the black-
and-white appearence.

## We see with our brain, not with our eyes

Daylight is not uniform in its composition, but instead undergoes constant **change** according to the time of year, weather conditions and geographical location. Human perception filters these variations out on grounds of efficiency – a sheet of white paper always appears white, even though it is only really so when seen in perfect lighting.

Even with artificial lighting, which may in some cases comprise a broad spectrum of wavelengths, the sheet of paper remains white as far as our perception is concerned.
Any tinge of colour is filtered out by our perceptive apparatus. It would appear that we rely heavily on ready-made templates for purposes of recognition.

**www.deutschebank.de**
Website for the eponymous
German bank.

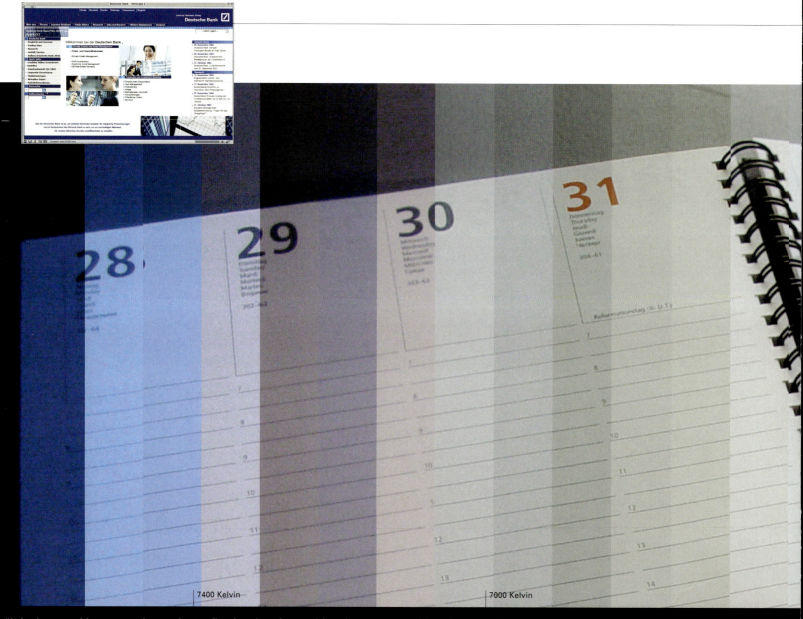

7400 Kelvin          7000 Kelvin

"It is the eye of ignorance that assigns a fixed and unchangeable colour to every object; beware of this stumbling block."
Paul Gauguin

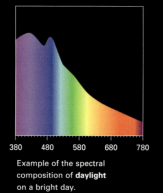

Example of the spectral
composition of **daylight**
on a bright day.

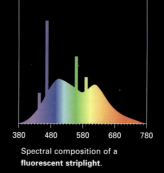

Spectral composition of a
**fluorescent striplight**.

24

The lens of the camera, on the other hand, captures light conditions as they really are. The light settings on film material are adjusted so as to minimise these tinges of colour. With digital cameras, there is a whiteness regulator, which fine-tunes the camera as appropriate to different light conditions.

"Now I really feel the landscape, I can be bold and include every tone of blue and pink: it's enchanting, it's delicious."

Claude Monet

see also pages 148I149

Conversely, by using a certain colour climate in the design phase, the lighting conditions of a particular time of year can be closely simulated. Colour filtering and colour correction enable graphic material to be tinged with a "morning" **blue tone**, communicating high energy, or with a **reddish orange**, inspiring associations with the sunset.

**www.havana-club.com**
Promotional website for
a liqueur.

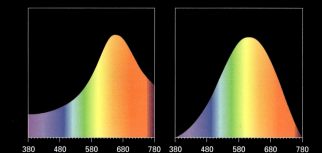

3200 Kelvin          2500 Kelvin

Each light source has its own composition, made up of various colours of the spectrum. The need for a basis on which to compare and contrast light sources has given rise to the term light temperature. This describes the colour affected by the light and is measured on the Kelvin scale. Daylight, for example, has a light temperature of 5500 K. This unit of measurement is not very representative, since blue, "cold" light has a high colour temperature, while yellow, "warm" light

380  480  580  680  780   380  480  580  680  780

**Colour memory and colour comparison**

Given **direct comparison** human perception is able to differentiate between thousands of colour nuances, however, the retention of colours is not quite so straightforward. Colours are not easily memorised and then recalled as and when they are needed.

Our colour memory is restricted to the coarse differentiation between colour family, saturation and brightness. Additionally, the context in which a colour appears strongly influences our impression of the colour. The problem becomes more acute on a **screen-based medium** where the light is generated by the display unit.

"They'll sell you thousands of greens. Veronese green and emerald green and cadmium green and any sort of green you like; but that particular green, never."

Pablo Picasso

If two identical blocks of colour are not viewed side by side, a kind of visual time delay starts to set in and the two blocks appear to be of different colours.

see also pages 50|51

"When we reflect on our past sentiments and affections, our thought is a faithful mirror, and copies its objects truly; but the colours which it employs are faint and dull, in comparison to those in which our original perceptions were clothed."

David Hume

The colour-correction function on the picture-processing program, Adobe Photoshop. Alternatives are presented in an easy-to-compare format, so as to cut down on decision time.

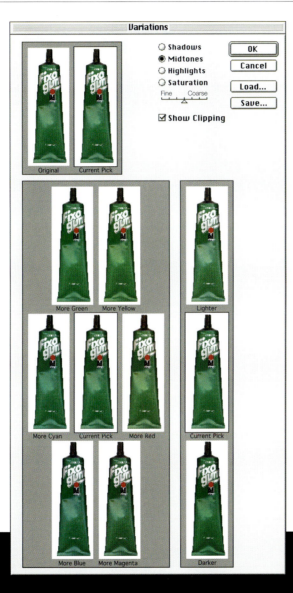

Even upon direct comparison, differences may still not show up: so-called **metameric colours** appear identical in certain light conditions and distinctly different in others.

The two blocks of colour in the area on the left are filled with exactly the same tone of green as the sample block.

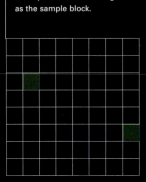

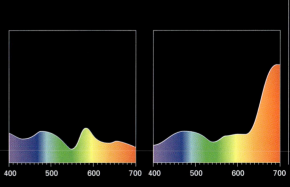

"'Yes,' I answered you last night, 'No,' this morning, Sir, I say. Colours seen by candle-light, Will not look the same by day."

Elizabeth Barrett Browning

**Nobody sees quite the same thing**

No two people see things in the same way. As well as the scope for manoeuvre in interpretation, which each perceptive apparatus makes different use of, there are also physiological differences which play a role.

Colour perception would appear to change with age. We tend to associate powerful, highly saturated colours with childhood. This may stem from a need for strong stimulation of the visual and perceptive apparatus during the development phase.

"When three people are of the same mind, yellow dirt can be turned into gold."
Chinese proverb

With age, the eye's lens becomes yellowed, leading to a shift in the visual spectrum towards yellow. Our perceptive apparatus filters this shift out. At the same time, our perception seems to become more sophisticated and prefers more subtle colours.

SiBEL

"I know for sure that I have an instinct for colour, and that it will come to me more and more, that painting is in the very marrow of my bones."
Vincent van Gogh

In the design stage, the possibility of colour-vision

The condition known as "colour blindness" can either
affect the green/red area, the blue/yellow area or the
complete spectrum and distort the viewer's sense
of colour to varying degrees. In digital applications,

Comparatively speaking, human perception is imprecise and sluggish. Details so small, they fall within a **viewing angle** of 2° or less, tend to disappear. For finer details to be picked out, the viewing distance has to be reduced. So as to compensate for the blind spot and to make the best use of the receptors on the retina, the eye is in constant motion, resulting in a slight toing and froing of the line of vision. This is the cause of several **visual illusions**, including that of the flicker effect.

The term **optical illusion** is misleading and incorrect, since this is a phenomenon belonging to visual perception. A more accurate term would be **visual illusion**.

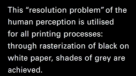

This "resolution problem" of the human perception is utilised for all printing processes: through rasterization of black on white paper, shades of grey are achieved.

Colour printing is based on the same principle: here individual dots of cyan, magenta, yellow and black combine to create a gamut of colours.

CRTs work in a similar fashion: three adjacent dots which are either red, green or blue create any blend of colours through their varied intensity.

The eye's sluggishness can even result in the perception of movement that isn't really there, a fact without which, the invention of the film would never have been possible. Moving film makes use of 24 different, yet similar, picture frames per second.
To create an **impression of movement**, much less is required, as we know from flip-book cartoons.

"Although the poet has as wide a choice of subjects as the painter, his creations fail to afford as much satisfaction to mankind as do paintings... if the poet serves the understanding by way of the ear, the painter does so by the eye, which is the nobler sense."

Leonardo da Vinci

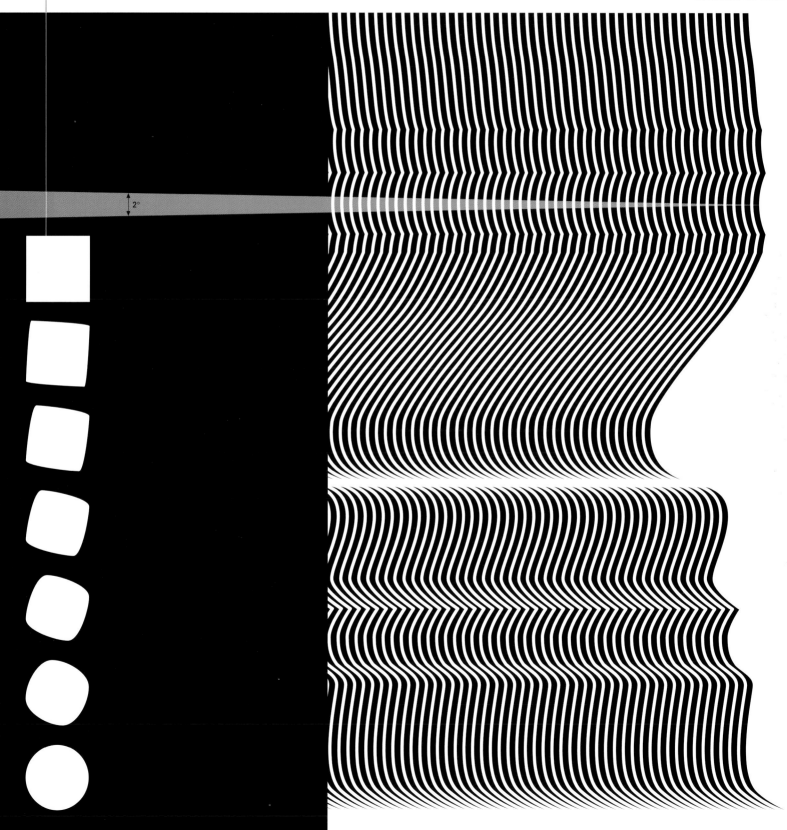

2°

# The Order of Colour

1 2 **3** 4 5 6 7 8 9

How are colours ordered? What criteria and parameters
are available for doing this? Is there a universally
accepted system and, if so, who first came up with or
discovered it?
This chapter clarifies some of the terminology and
provides an introduction to the most important ways
of ordering colours.

## Ordering colours

Philosophers, scientists and artists have for centuries been working to develop some kind of logical system whereby colours might be ordered. The various systems that have emerged begin by establishing relationships between the primary colours. Geometric diagrams based on triangles, squares, hexagons or **circles** are helpful visual aids for demonstrating these relationships.

It is not so much the order in which the colours are arranged but rather the weight assigned to them within a particular system that differentiates the systems.

Thus we find models based on measured equal distance between hues and others based on perceived equal distance.

see also pages 14|15

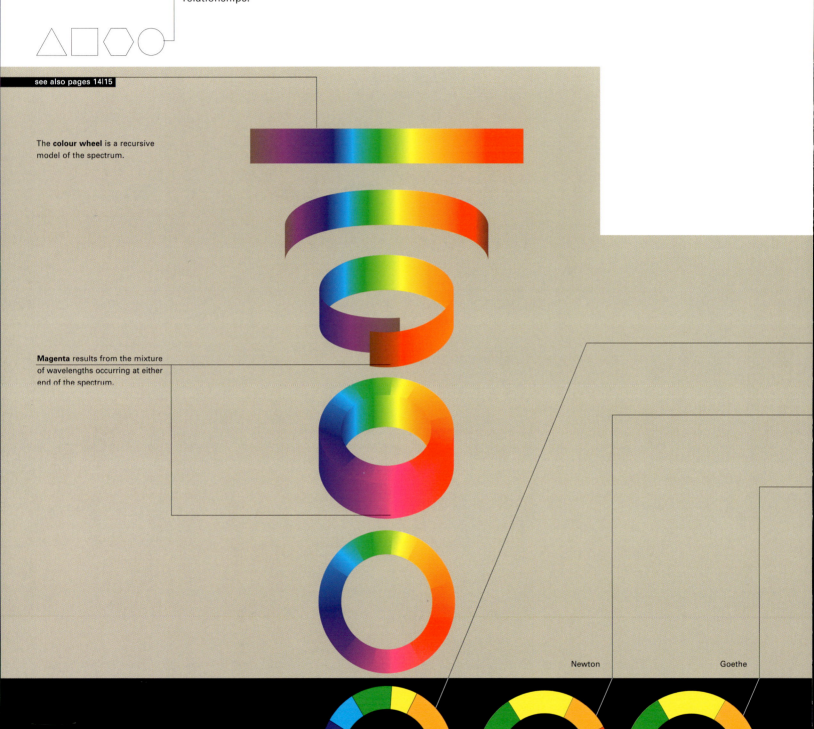

The **colour wheel** is a recursive model of the spectrum.

**Magenta** results from the mixture of wavelengths occurring at either end of the spectrum.

Newton

Goethe

see also pages 48|49

The question of which three colours comprise the **primary colours** depends on the **method of mixture** being used – for a light-based or **additive** colour mixture, they would be red, green and blue while for a pigment-based, **subtractive** colour mixture, yellow, magenta and cyan. The **secondary colours** are to be found about halfway between any two primary colours and again differ according to the method of mixture. **Tertiary colours** is the term used to refer to the tones located between each primary and secondary colour.

What we refer to in the classical sense as primary colours are those which cannot be obtained through mixing other colours together. It would also be possible to designate as primary colours any set of colours that, in accordance with one's perception, are clearly defined and do not contain traces of another colour.

secondary colours

tertiary colours

Even the process of assigning names to colours is essentially arbitrary and can lead to misunderstandings. The following is a list of the most commonly used names on the colour wheel:

carmine
red-violet
magenta
violet
blue-violet
indigo
blue
ice blue
cyan
yellow-green
sea green
green
yellow
yellow-orange
orange
red-orange
red

Equidistantly structured colour wheels based on perception are least accurate to the actual distribution of the spectrum.

Itten

Küppers

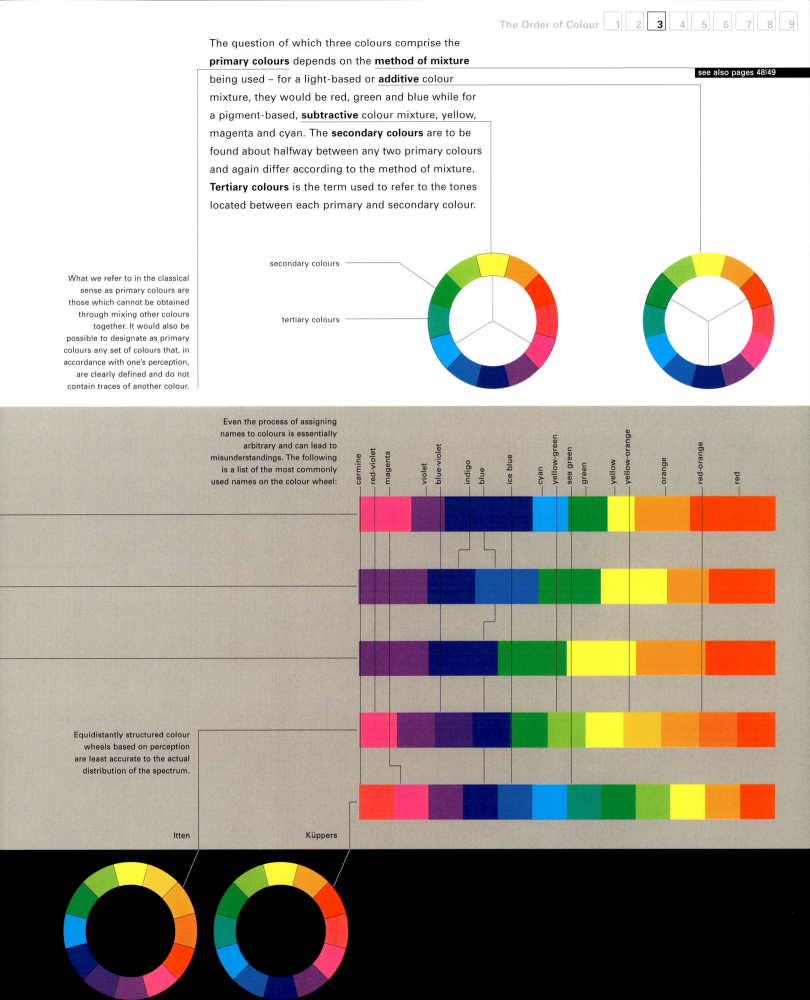

**Naming colours**

Each highly saturated, pure colour or hue on the colour wheel provides the basis for a **colour family**. A colour family may either encompass a wider or narrower range depending on the type of colour wheel presentation. Each family can be seen as a systematical variation on a hue. Saturation and brightness are two factors of a hue that may be varied.

All graduated variations within a colour family are one and the same hue.

The saturation or **chroma** of the colours in the colour wheel corresponds to 100%, the term "reduction of saturation" is used to describe a drop in the proportion of colour. The second parameter is the brightness or **value** of the colour. Despite already having its own intrinsic brightness – a pure yellow is brighter than a pure violet – a colour's brightness may be either increased or decreased by raising the proportion of white or black.

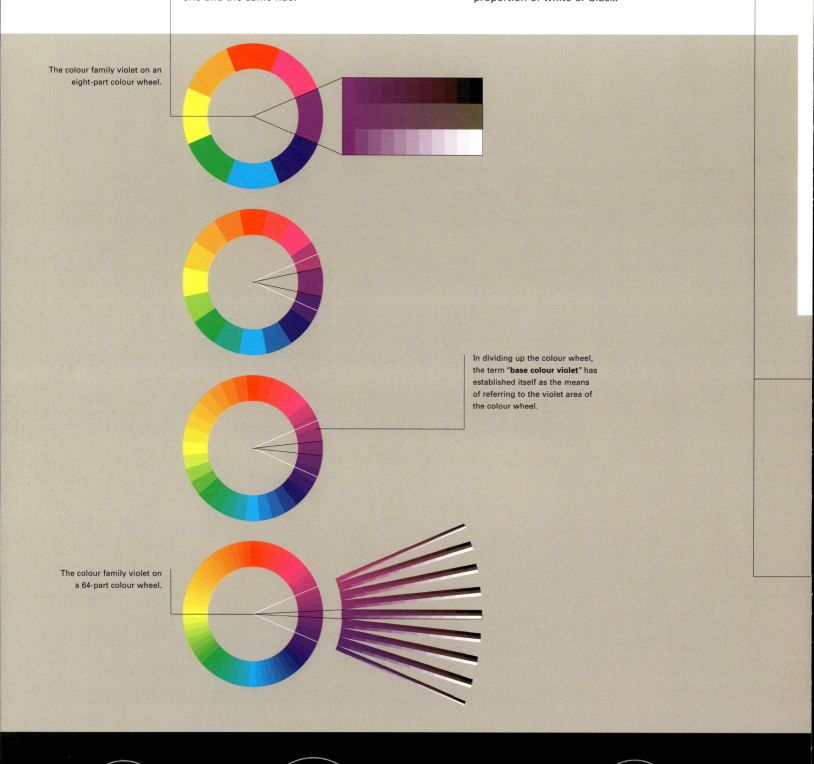

The colour family violet on an eight-part colour wheel.

In dividing up the colour wheel, the term "**base colour violet**" has established itself as the means of referring to the violet area of the colour wheel.

The colour family violet on a 64-part colour wheel.

della Porta

Aguilonius

ALBVS  FLAVVS  RVBEVS  CÆRVLEVS  NIGER

Kircher

1600

1650

A concept for structured ordering of the primary
colours and their corresponding colour families is
commonly known as a **colour system**.
The translation of such a colour system in the form
of colour samples is known as **colour order**.
It is worth noting that the terms colour system and
colour order are often used synonymously.

Since the parameters colour tone, saturation and
brightness are unsuited to a two-dimensional
representation, the term **colour space** has come to
be used to describe the way of representing
that relationship.

hue

tints

tones

shades

greys

Saturation 100%

Saturation 0%

The reduction in saturation
is what causes the achromatic
or greyish **tones** within
a colour family.

Proportion of white 100%
Brightness 100%

An increase in the proportion
of white does not mean
a reduction in saturation,
colours lightened by adding
white are known as **tints**.

Proportion of black 100%
Brightness   0%

An increase in the proportion
of black does not mean
a reduction in saturation,
colours darkened by adding
black are known as **shades**.

## Colour space ordered according to proportion of black or white

The need to visually represent the various colours along with the saturation and brightness graduations that comprise each colour family has led to the development of three-dimensional colour models. These systems allow the different parameters to be represented on separate axes within a virtual space. The resultant form, be it a sphere, cylinder or hourglass shape, includes all the colours of the system.

What these shapes have in common is that they all display rotational symmetry around a central axis. This axis represents an **achromatic scale** of grey shades ranging between the two poles, black and white.

In this colour model, colours with **equal proportions of white** are on the same level.

Proportion of white 100%

Taking the hue as a basis, going upwards from the mid-point, the proportion of white increases whilst going downwards, the proportion of black increases. This type of colour space does not take the levels of intrinsic brightness into account.

Colours of equal saturation are equal distant from the central axis.

Proportion of black 100%

Mayer

Lambert

Goethe
Runge

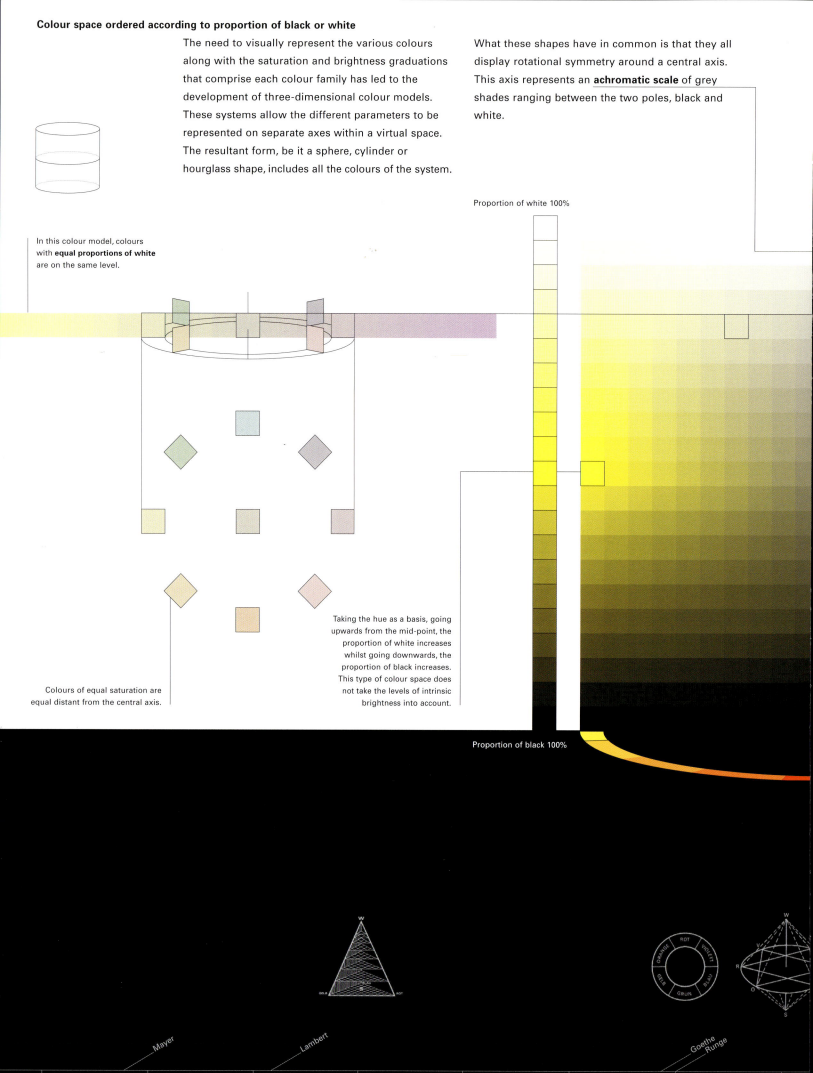

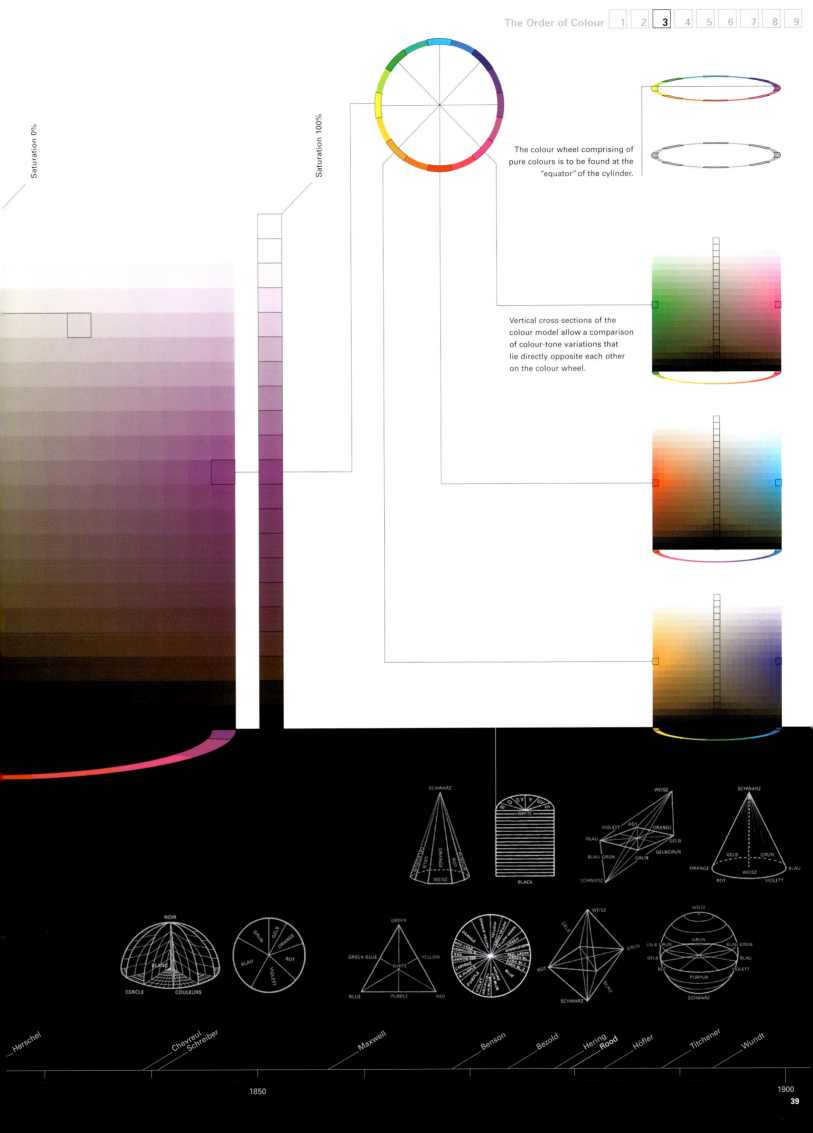

Saturation 0%

Saturation 100%

The colour wheel comprising of pure colours is to be found at the "equator" of the cylinder.

Vertical cross-sections of the colour model allow a comparison of colour-tone variations that lie directly opposite each other on the colour wheel.

SCHWARZ

WEISZ

SCHWARZ

VIOLETT  ROT  ORANGE

BLAU  GELB

BLAU GRUN  GELBGRUN

SCHWARZ  GRUN

GELB  GRUN

ORANGE  WEISZ  BLAU

ROT  VIOLETT

GRÜNROT  GELB  PURPUR  ROT

ORANGE  WEISZ

WHITE

R  O  O  Y  V  V  G  Y  G

BLACK

NOIR

GRÜN  GELB

ORANGE

BLAU  ROT

VIOLETT

BLANC

CERCLE  COULEURS

GREEN

GREEN BLUE  YELLOW

WHITE

BLUE  RED

PURPLE

ORANGE  ORANGE YELLOW  NEPTUN  GREEN YELLOW

RED LEAD  GREEN

VERMILLON  EMERALD

RED  GREEN BLUE

CARMINE  GREEN BL.1

R.PURPLE  GREEN BL.2

VIOLETT  LIGHT BLUE

VIOLET  ULTRAMAR.  BLUE

WEISZ

GELB  GRUN

ROT  GRUN

BLAU

SCHWARZ

WEISZ

GRUN

GELB GRUN  BLAU GRUN

GELB  BLAU

ROT  VIOLETT

PURPUR

SCHWARZ

Herschel

Chevreul
Schreiber

Maxwell

Benson

Bezold

Hering  **Rood**

Höfler

Titchener

Wundt

1850

1900

**39**

## Colour space ordered according to brightness

Some more recent colour models also take the intrinsic brightness of the colours into account. This results in complex, often irregular three-dimensional shapes. Once again, all the colours are arranged in a circle around a central axis that represents a scale of grey shades. However, the form is stretched so as to account for variations in colour range of the base colours. Thus yellow includes more light tones than violet, which offers a correspondingly wider palette of darker tones.

Colour models that are arranged according to saturation are most commonly used for pigment colours because the user can look up the components of a colour mix at a glance. Colour models arranged according to brightness, on the other hand, are more suitable for use with screen-based media.

In this colour model, colours of **equal brightness** are to be found at the same level.

Colours with the same level of saturation are arranged in an irregular ring formation around the central axis. The distance between a colour and the central axis may vary and depends on the range of tones at a particular level of brightness.

Each hue is assigned a position on the central axis of grey shades according to intrinsic brightness. Thus yellow, which has a high level of intrinsic brightness, is positioned well towards the lighter end of the scale than violet, which has a low intrinsic brightness.

Brightness 100%

Brightness 0%

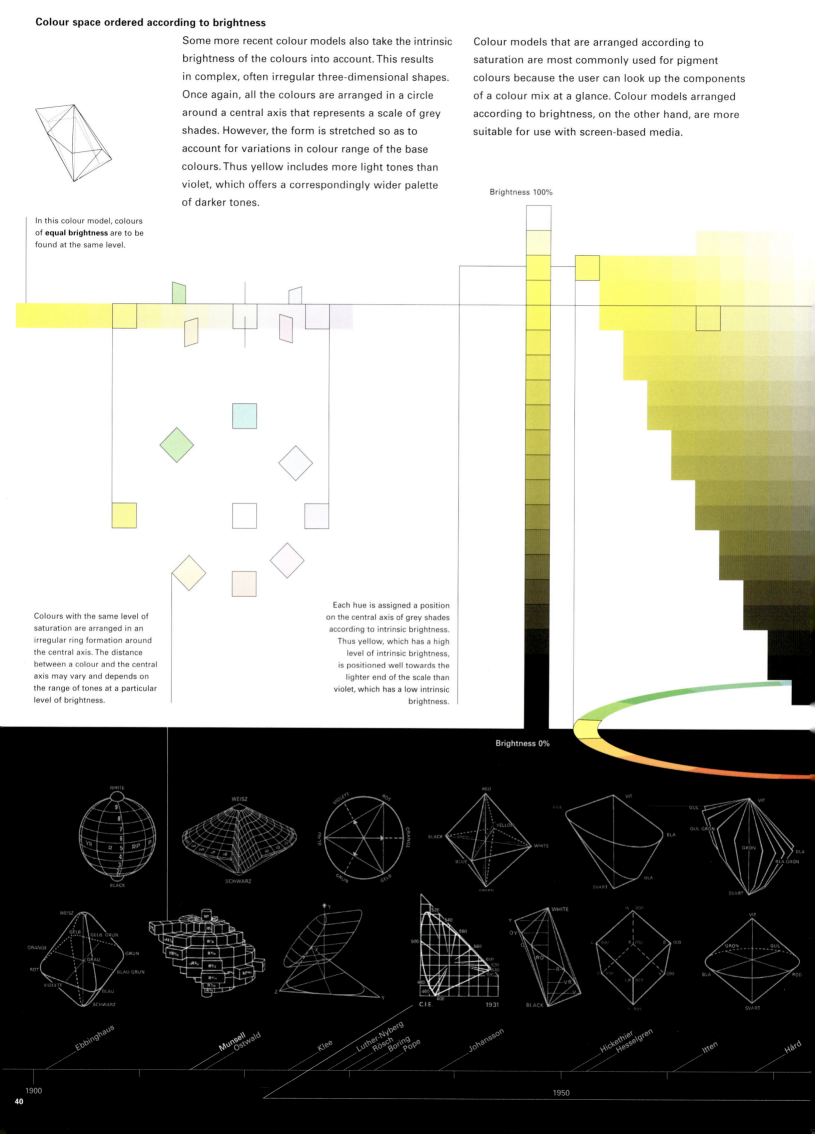

Ebbinghaus    Munsell Ostwald    Klee    Luther-Nyberg Rösch Boring Pope    Johansson    Hickethier Hesselgren    Itten    Hård

1900    1950

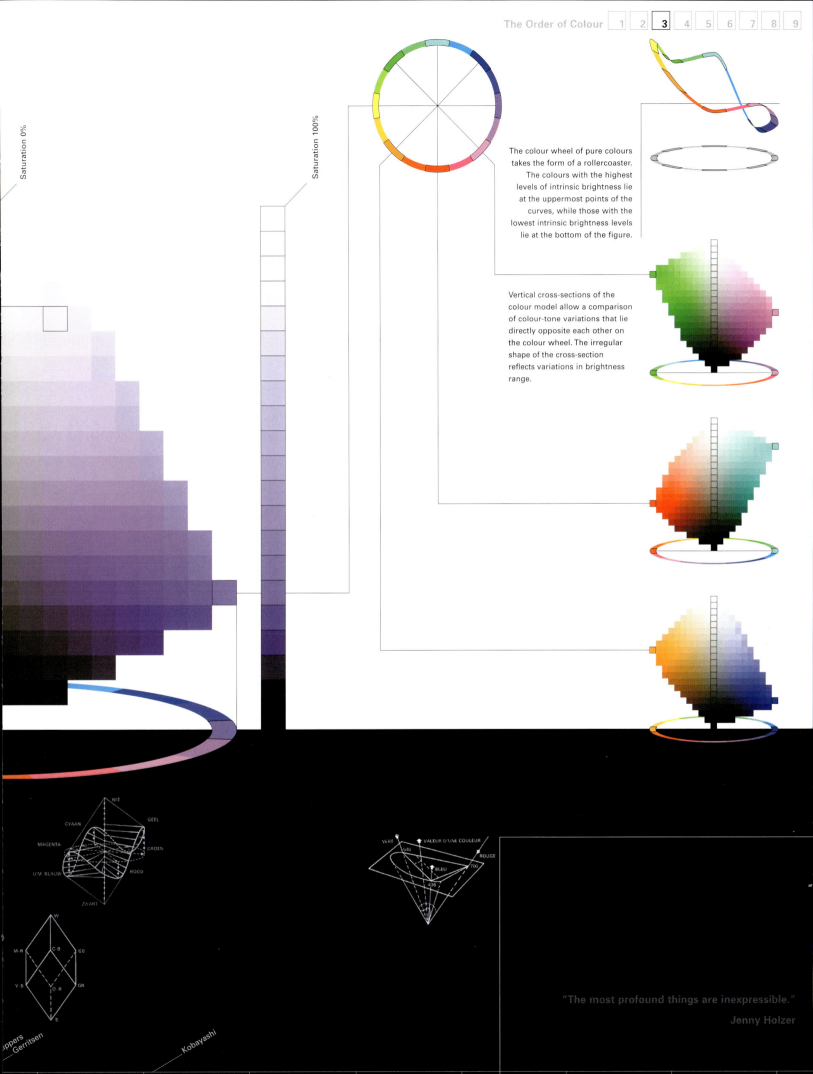

Saturation 0%

Saturation 100%

The colour wheel of pure colours takes the form of a rollercoaster. The colours with the highest levels of intrinsic brightness lie at the uppermost points of the curves, while those with the lowest intrinsic brightness levels lie at the bottom of the figure.

Vertical cross-sections of the colour model allow a comparison of colour-tone variations that lie directly opposite each other on the colour wheel. The irregular shape of the cross-section reflects variations in brightness range.

WIT

CYAAN GEEL

MAGENTA GROEN

U.M. BLAUW ROOD

ZWART

W

M-R C-B GB

V-B GR

O R

S

VERT VALEUR D'UNE COULEUR
540
ROUGE
BLEU 700
436

Uppers
Gerritsen

Kobayashi

"The most profound things are inexpressible."
Jenny Holzer

## The good old shoe sole

CIE = Commission Internationale de l`Eclairage or the International Commission on Illumination.

The **CIE** or "shoe sole" model has established itself as the standard colour model for computer purposes due to the fact that it includes all the colours of the spectrum visible to the human eye. The pure colours of the spectrum are arranged in a formation resembling the outline of the sole of a shoe.

The reason for the colour model's irregular shape is that it is based on curves which are used to compute how much of x, y and z should be mixed together to generate a **metamerism** of any visible colour. These curves are corresponding to the sensitivity of the **three types of cone** that make up the human eye – each wavelength range is measured by one of the three axes of the model.

see also pages 26|27

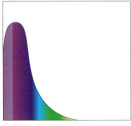

cones sensitive to blue

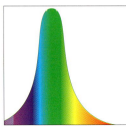

cones sensitive to green

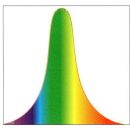

cones sensitive to red

"Artists can colour the sky red because they know it's blue. Those of us who aren't artists must colour things the way they really are or people might think we're stupid."

Jules Feiffer

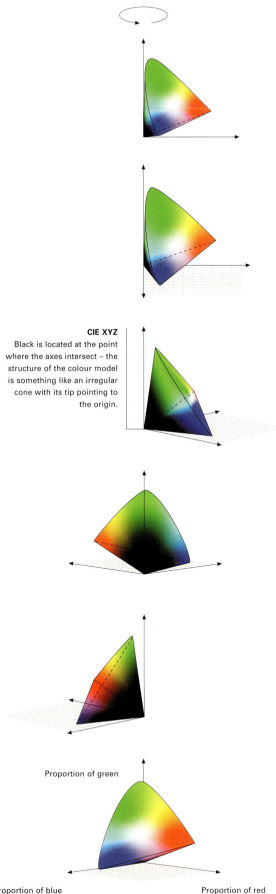

**CIE XYZ**
Black is located at the point where the axes intersect – the structure of the colour model is something like an irregular cone with its tip pointing to the origin.

Proportion of green

Proportion of blue

Proportion of red

The shoe sole is often reduced to two dimensions for the purpose of diagrams. It is possible to derive the third component through calculations as long as both of the other two components are known. For any colour, the designer is able to look up the exact composition in terms of the three primary colours of the additive colour scheme, the proportions of which correspond to the coordinates in space.
Tones and shades are not, however, represented in this model.

This chromatic diagram offers a comparison of the various colour profiles, making it possible to identify which areas of colour lie outside the **range** of a particular medium.
The colour-temperature scale is represented as a curve within the colour spectrum.

see also pages 64|65

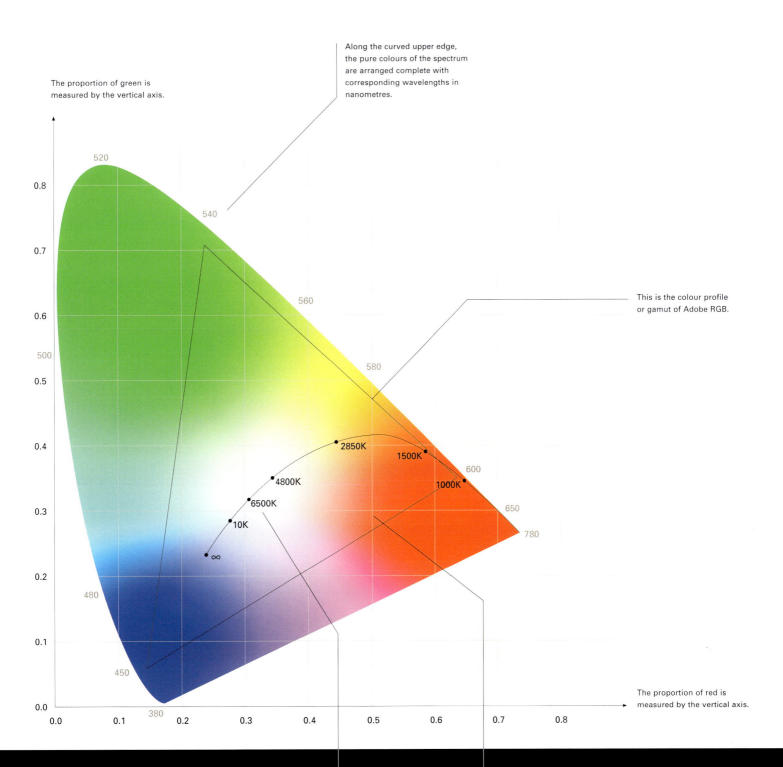

Along the curved upper edge, the pure colours of the spectrum are arranged complete with corresponding wavelengths in nanometres.

The proportion of green is measured by the vertical axis.

This is the colour profile or gamut of Adobe RGB.

The proportion of red is measured by the vertical axis.

The proportion of blue is calculable from the components red and green since red, green and blue together result in a value of 1.

Here, the visual representation of colour temperature is shown in degrees Kelvin. The white point, as it is known, is located at 6500K and is comparable to daylight.

This tone has a green element of 0.3 and a red element of 0.5, the blue element of the colour's composition must therefore be 0.2.

## Colour and space

The fact that colours have varying levels of intrinsic brightness is of particular importance on the screen. We perceive yellow as being a lighter colour and blue as being quite a lot darker. Such variations in intrinsic brightness become even more pronounced on the screen. This self-illuminating medium not only offers a completely different **range of colours**, it also alters the intrinsic brightness of the colours and consequently the way in which the viewer is affected by them.

Translating a colour into a grey tone of equal brightness is a helpful way of judging the level of intrinsic brightness.

Contrasting the eight basic colours on the screen is a good way of illustrating how intrinsic brightness changes from colour to colour. Yellow represents a greyscale value of 10%.

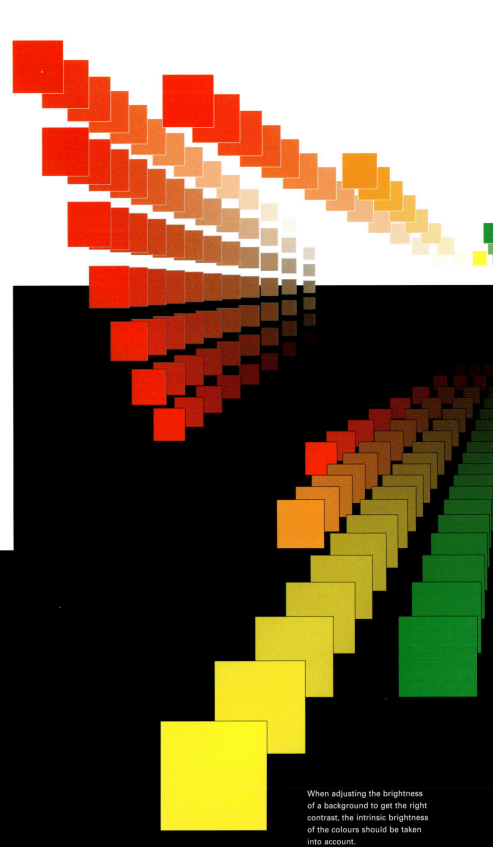

When adjusting the brightness of a background to get the right contrast, the intrinsic brightness of the colours should be taken into account.

"I will concentrate on the beauty of one blue hill in the distance, and for me, that moment will be eternity."

Alice Walker

see also pages 48|49

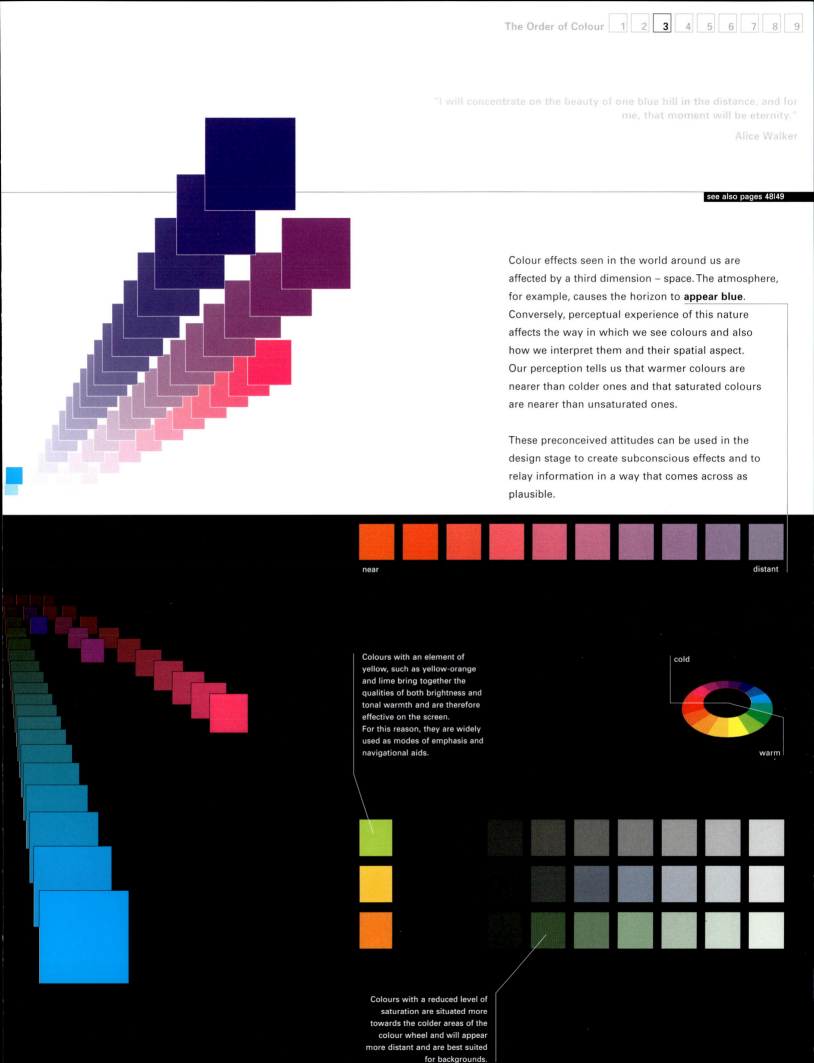

Colour effects seen in the world around us are affected by a third dimension – space. The atmosphere, for example, causes the horizon to **appear blue**. Conversely, perceptual experience of this nature affects the way in which we see colours and also how we interpret them and their spatial aspect. Our perception tells us that warmer colours are nearer than colder ones and that saturated colours are nearer than unsaturated ones.

These preconceived attitudes can be used in the design stage to create subconscious effects and to relay information in a way that comes across as plausible.

near                                                                distant

Colours with an element of yellow, such as yellow-orange and lime bring together the qualities of both brightness and tonal warmth and are therefore effective on the screen.
For this reason, they are widely used as modes of emphasis and navigational aids.

cold

warm

Colours with a reduced level of saturation are situated more towards the colder areas of the colour wheel and will appear more distant and are best suited for backgrounds.

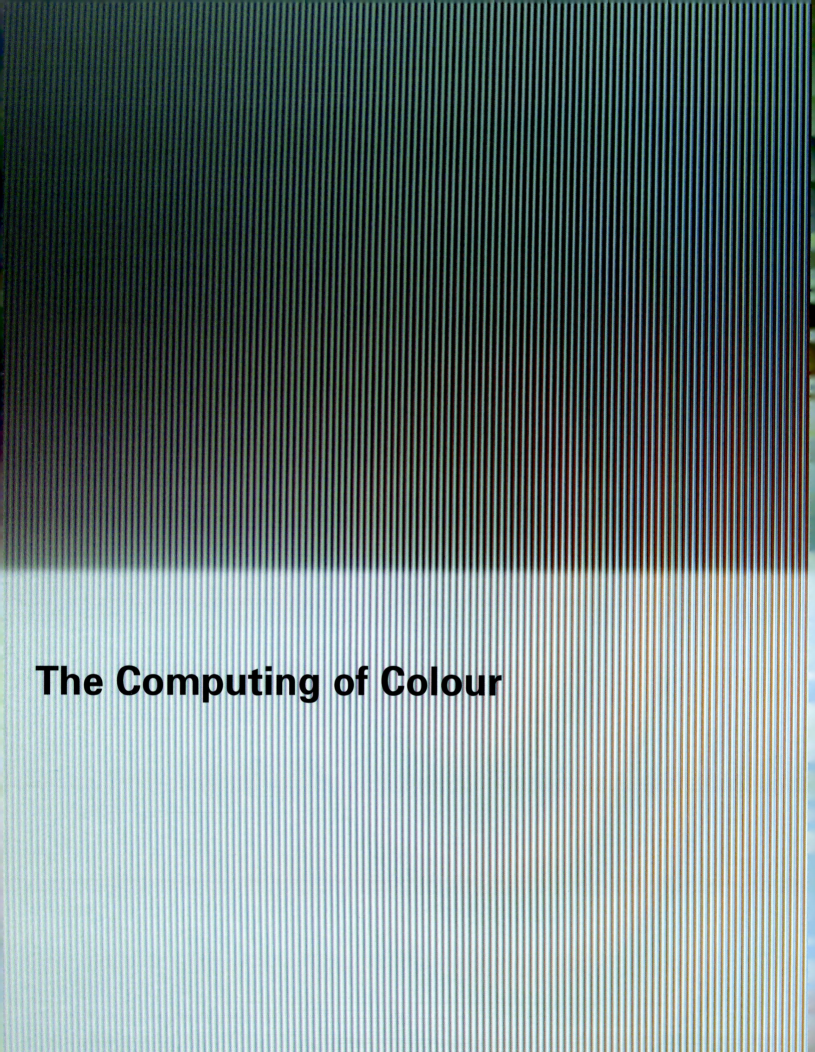

# The Computing of Colour

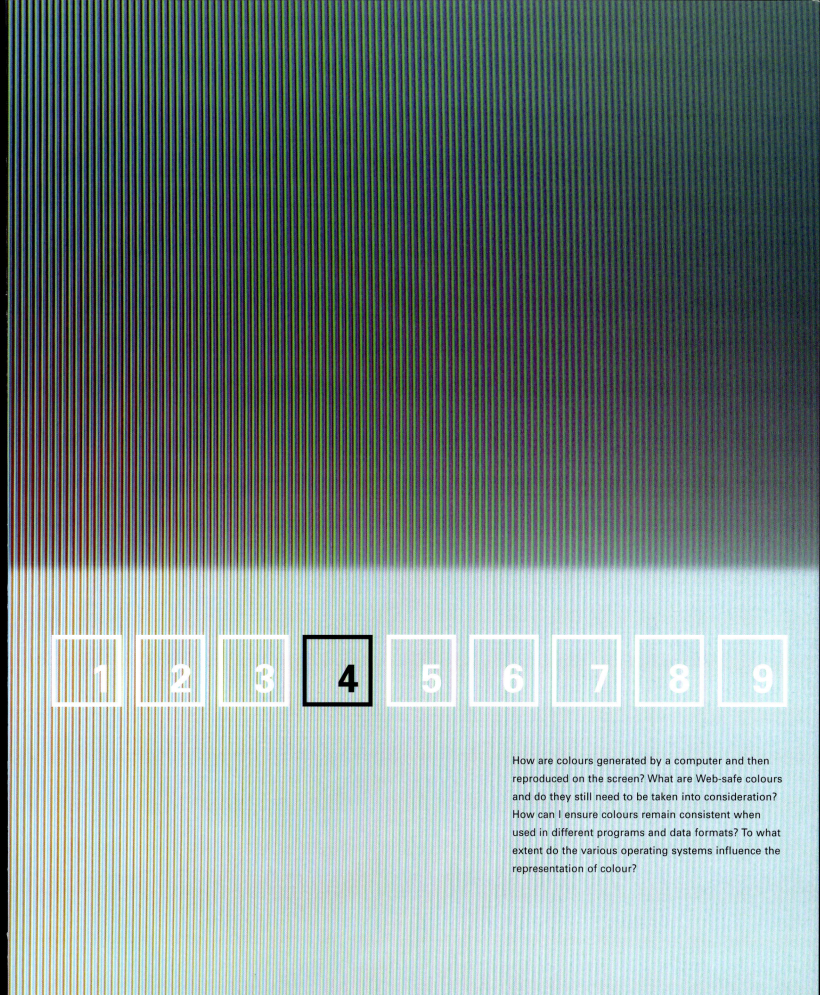

How are colours generated by a computer and then reproduced on the screen? What are Web-safe colours and do they still need to be taken into consideration? How can I ensure colours remain consistent when used in different programs and data formats? To what extent do the various operating systems influence the representation of colour?

**The additive colour system**

Like a television a computer display works using light-based colours. The three primary colours of the additive colour system – red, green and blue – are mixed to produce all the other colours. This is called the additive colour system because it involves adding light at various wavelengths.

The additive colour system is not, however, capable of producing all the colours of the spectrum because it uses only red, green and blue – mixing these three colours produces **metamer colours**. This makes perfect sense when one considers that no light of other wavelengths is available and so the result is in fact a close approximation derived through mixture.

see also pages 26|27

"Computing is not about computers any more. It is about living."
Nicholas Negroponte

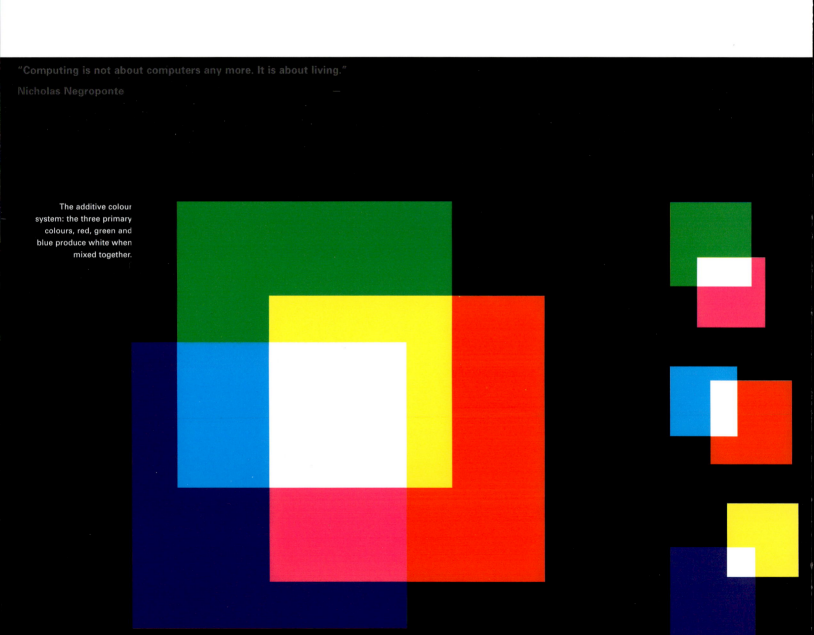

The additive colour system: the three primary colours, red, green and blue produce white when mixed together.

Yellow, cyan and magenta are the secondary colours of the additive colour system. They are lighter than the primary colours and also comprise the primary colours of the **subtractive colour system**. Mixing all three primary colours of the additive colour system gives white.

The subtractive colour system: the three primary colours are yellow, cyan and magenta

see also pages 64|65

The CIE colour model shows the range of colours or gamut visible to the human eye. Transposed on to this diagram is the gamut a computer screen is able to produce. These parameters vary according to the type of screen.

"If it weren't for Philo T. Farnsworth, inventor of the television, we'd still be eating frozen radio dinners."

Johnny Carson

While most of us are familiar with how the subtractive colour system works, the principles underlying the additive colour system are harder to comprehend.

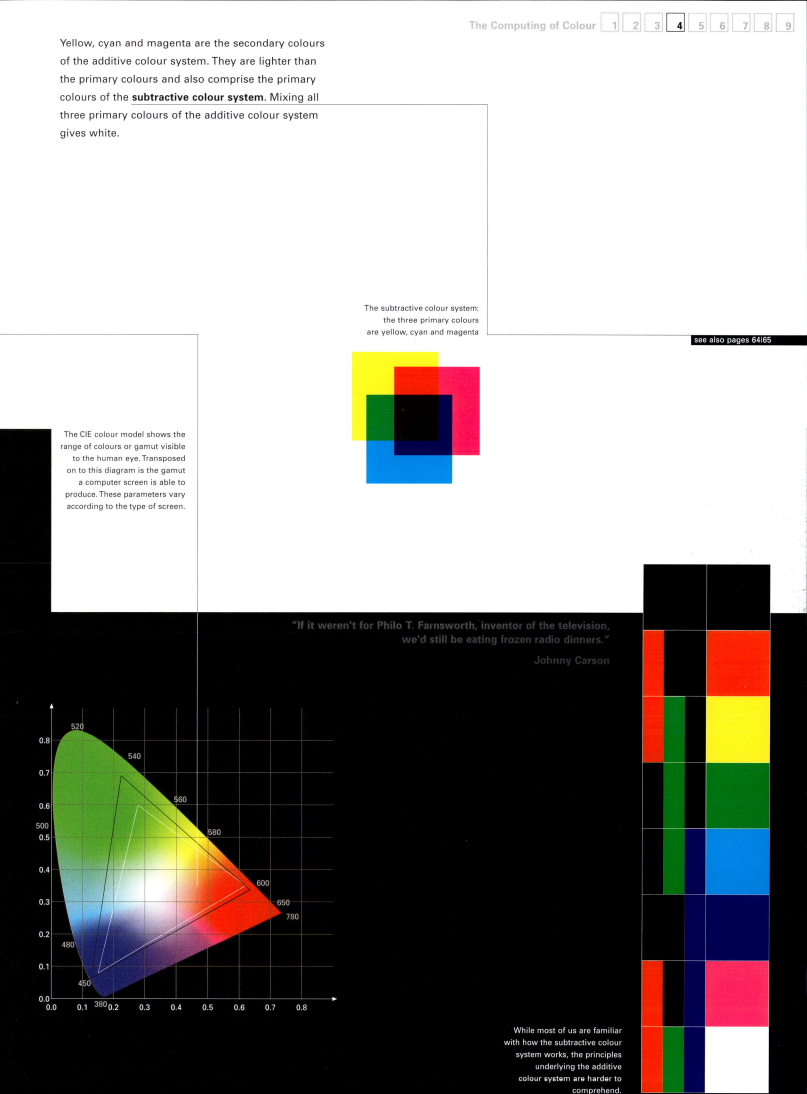

## Screen-based systems of output

The appearence of colours on the screen is subject to several factors. Technical specifications, particularly those of the display unit, play a deciding role, as do the operating system, the program being used and time of day or play of light on the screen.

Today, the most widely used screen is still the cathode ray tube. These units tend to give off high intensities of light making them effective even in daylight.

Using a diverted **stream of electrons** confined within a vacuum, a picture is built up line by line. The frequency at which the picture is created is measured in Megahertz. The higher the frequency, the better the end result – upwards of around 100 Mghz, screen flicker is no longer visible. No matter what precautions are taken, looking at a screen for long periods of time will put strain on the eyes.

One stream of electrons per colour is projected through a shadow mask and on to the phosphor-coated inner surface of the monitor to produce one of the three light-based colours. This mask ensures that each beam only makes contact with and illuminates the phosphor dot for which it is intended.

Each set of triple colours is called a triad and equivalent to a pixel on the screen. Pixel = picture element

Makes of CRT monitors vary in their specifications. Displays that use shadow masks to produce dots on screen...

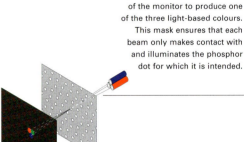

...as well as displays that use aperture grill wires to produce dots. By letting more light through, aperture grills offer higher levels of brilliance.

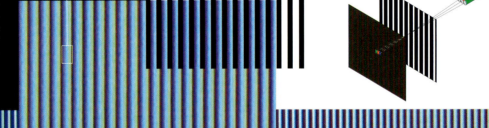

"Never trust a computer you can't throw out a window."

Steve Wozniak

LCD screens, which are distinguished by their flicker-free picture quality do not, however, offer rich contrasts and are highly dependent on the light conditions.

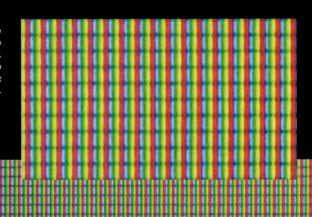

**Liquid Crystal Displays** are becoming more and more popular and, due to higher production volume, affordable too. On LCD units, an image is represented by cells which can be individually activated.
The picture on screen is static and updates are only necessary at those points on the screen which require updating. This is what makes LCD screens flicker-free. The speed at which the individual cells can be updated is still slightly lower than the frequency level for conventional CRT screens.

The lower levels of light emitted and the narrower viewing angle are – together with the price – reasons why LCD screens have not yet succeeded in completely taking over the market.

To help minimise colour **inconsistencies**, a standard calibration scale has become the normal way of measuring light. This scale sets the white point, i.e. daylight at around 6500° Kelvin. Actual levels of **contrast and brightness** produced are two factors separating the most commonly used computer platforms, PC and Mac, particularly with CRT monitors.

see also pages 60|61

Each screen has its own individual colour profile. Even using a different type of phosphor to coat the matt glass plate is enough to influence how colours appear on the screen.

"Without lights, it's radio."  Tantris Hardee

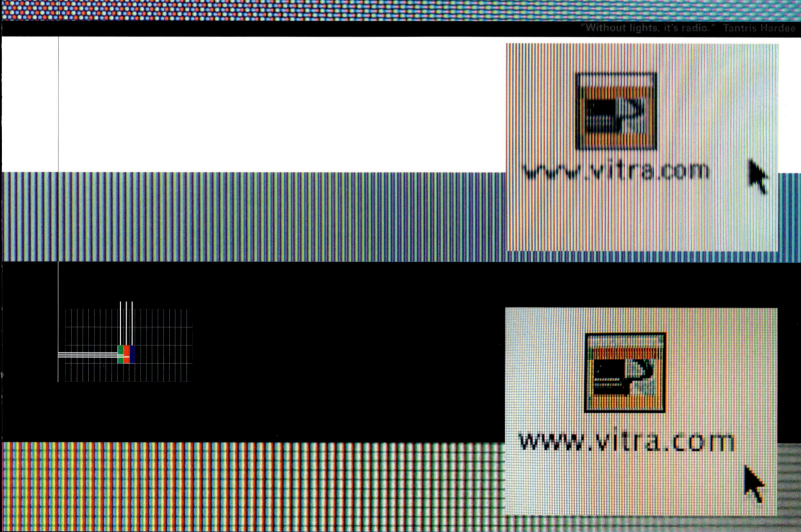

# What is colour depth?

The first computers operated using one colour. An electron beam activated the phosphor-coating of the screen causing characters – normally at least green or amber in colour – to appear on the black matt-glass plate.

The success of PCs has been built on the increasing user friendliness offered by applications such as desktop publishing. Such applications simulate printed paper, i.e. the whole screen is illuminated while the text itself emits no light. But here too, the first applications had to be content with black-and-white representations. More elaborated **halftone** techniques such as the Floyd-Steinberg Dither produced greyscales using visual colour mixtures.

The next evolutionary step was the introduction of 8-bit, which enables the use of **256 shades** of grey or colour representations using 256 colours either pre-set by the operating system or selected by the user. Here too, dithering allows to virtually expand the palette.

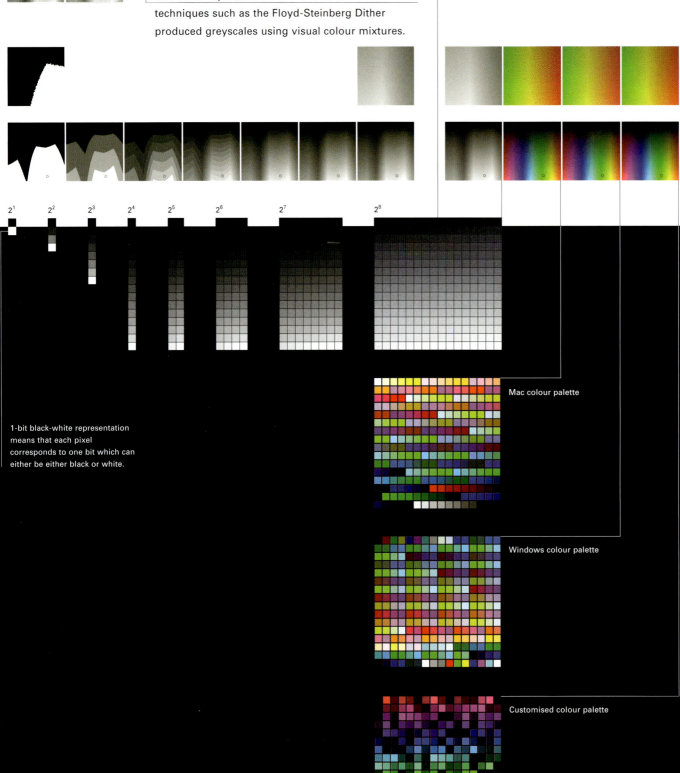

$2^1$  $2^2$  $2^3$  $2^4$  $2^5$  $2^6$  $2^7$  $2^8$

1-bit black-white representation means that each pixel corresponds to one bit which can either be either black or white.

Mac colour palette

Windows colour palette

Customised colour palette

Most operating systems now support 24-bit or 32-bit colour depth, that's **16.7 million** colours! This uses up a lot of memory, especially in combination with constant increases in display sizes.

To economise, displays with 16-bit colour depth, which can represent **thousands of colours**, are still in use.

With a 32-bit colour depth, the chunks of 8-bit are used in different ways depending on the colour model – in the CMYK model, a chunk of 8-bit is dedicated to each colour, while in the RGB model, the fourth chunk is set aside for representing 256 transparency levels.

$2^{15}=2^5 \times 2^5 \times 2^5$

$2^{16}=2^5 \times 2^6 \times 2^5$

$2^{24}=2^8=x2^8 \times 2^8$

$2^{32}=2^8 \times 2^8 \times 2^8 \times 2^8$

$2^{32}=2^8 \times 2^8 \times 2^8 \times 2^8$

15-bit colour depth or High Colour on the Macintosh offers 5 bits per colour channel or 32,768 colours.

24-bit colour depth or True Colour uses 8 bits (256 colours) per colour channel and is able to represent 16,777,216 colours.

16-bit colour depth or High Colour on a PC offers 5 x 6 x 5 bits or 65,536 colours.

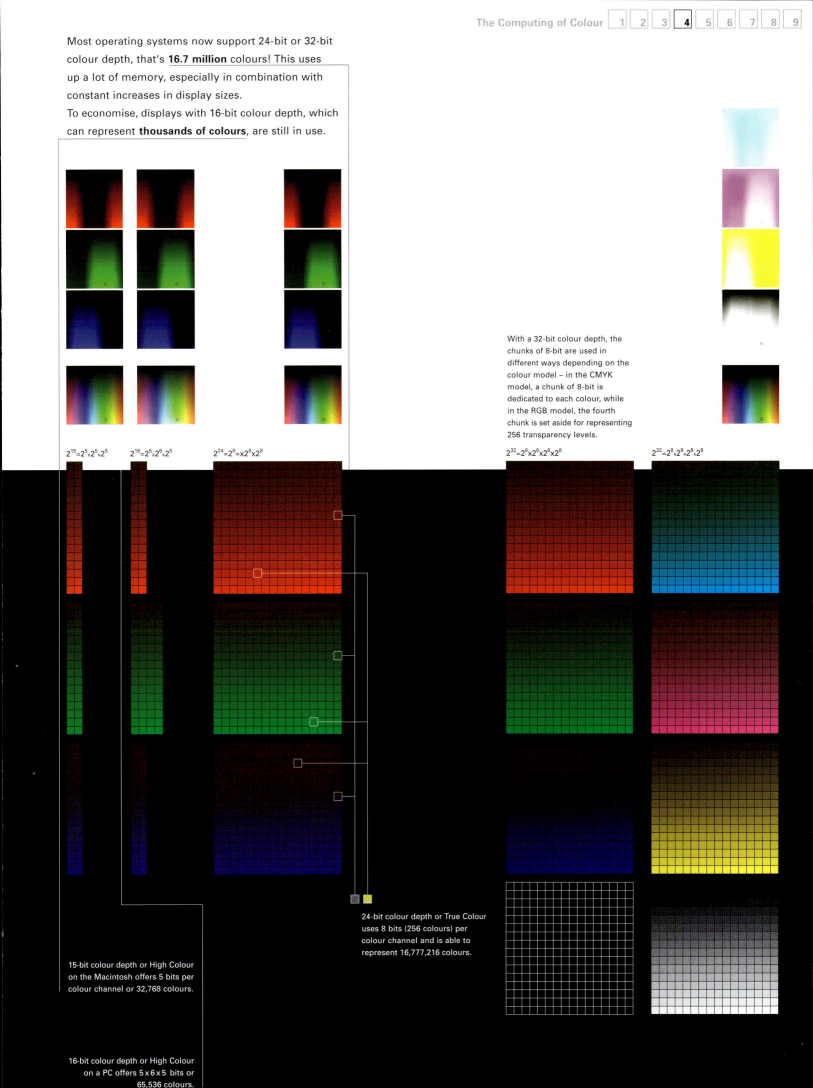

## How to choose a colour

There are various colour models available on the computer to aid the choice of colour. Many models are based on a **cube-shaped colour space** within which colours can be mapped and given coordinates. This kind of simplified model does not correspond to the classical colour space (e.g. **Munsell**) and tends to result in the contraction or stretching of certain colour familes.

see also pages 40|41

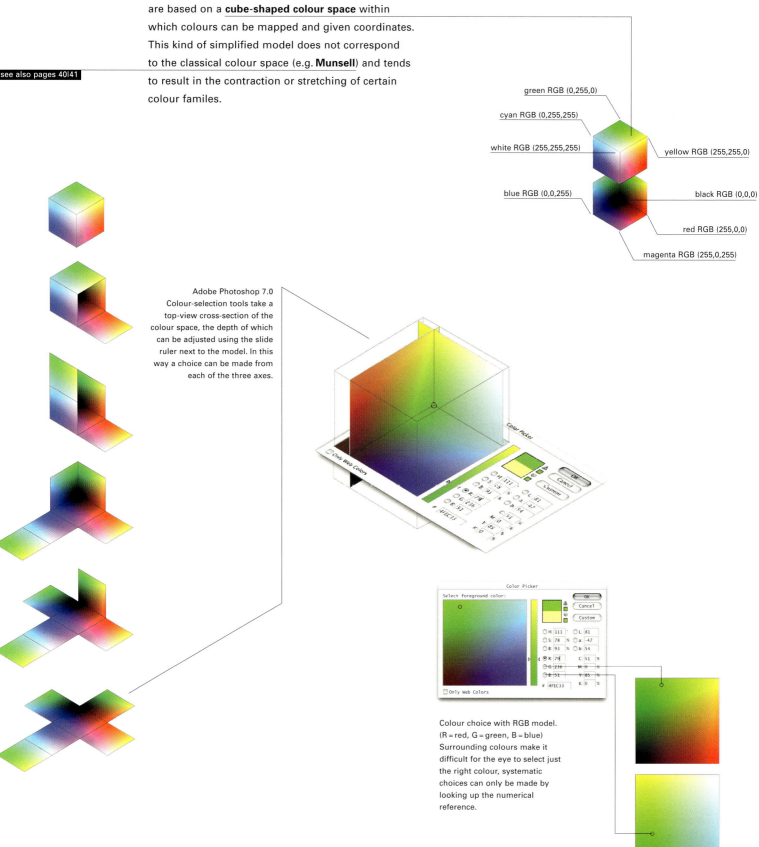

green RGB (0,255,0)

cyan RGB (0,255,255)

white RGB (255,255,255)

yellow RGB (255,255,0)

blue RGB (0,0,255)

black RGB (0,0,0)

red RGB (255,0,0)

magenta RGB (255,0,255)

Adobe Photoshop 7.0 Colour-selection tools take a top-view cross-section of the colour space, the depth of which can be adjusted using the slide ruler next to the model. In this way a choice can be made from each of the three axes.

Colour choice with RGB model. (R = red, G = green, B = blue) Surrounding colours make it difficult for the eye to select just the right colour, systematic choices can only be made by looking up the numerical reference.

The **HSV model** is about the best guide to colour selection because it minimises any misleading **simultaneous contrasts**. A colour tone can only really be judged if it is represented in a big enough quantity, which is why a good-quality colour-selection tool will present the user with larger samples.

see also pages 78|79

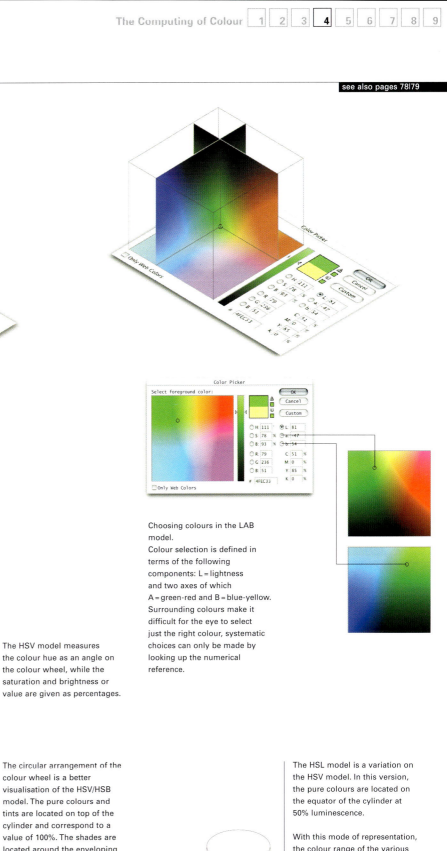

Colour choice in HSB/HSV model.
(H = hue, S = saturation, B = brightness, V = value.)
The colour family is selected from the colour wheel using the slide rule. Saturation and brightness of the selected colour are shown in the display box. This system enables a very precise choice of colour because the monochromatic range offered is all but unaffected by distortion-causing contrasts.

The HSV model measures the colour hue as an angle on the colour wheel, while the saturation and brightness or value are given as percentages.

Choosing colours in the LAB model.
Colour selection is defined in terms of the following components: L = lightness and two axes of which A = green-red and B = blue-yellow. Surrounding colours make it difficult for the eye to select just the right colour, systematic choices can only be made by looking up the numerical reference.

The circular arrangement of the colour wheel is a better visualisation of the HSV/HSB model. The pure colours and tints are located on top of the cylinder and correspond to a value of 100%. The shades are located around the enveloping surface. The saturation is measured radially. The brightness corresponds to the height of the cylinder.

The HSL model is a variation on the HSV model. In this version, the pure colours are located on the equator of the cylinder at 50% luminescence.

With this mode of representation, the colour range of the various colour families has undergone significant compression or stretching to ensure it fits the form of the model.
This model is often confused with the HSV/HSB model.

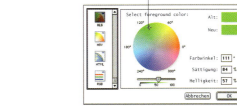

## What are Web-safe colours and what is the significance of FF33CC?

Web-safe colours are the **216 colours** forming the basis of the 8-bit palette which should appear the same regardless of the operating system or browser. They represent the lowest common denominator as far as net-suitable colours are concerned. Yet even these supposedly safe colours are not always consistent in appearance. Numerous tests have wittled this "safe" palette down to a collection of **22 colours**, leaving the designer with barely any choice.

Furthermore, incorrectly rounding a colour up or down may lead to inconsistencies between colours generated by HTML code and colours saved as image data. Displays only capable of working in high colour are particularly susceptible to deviations in colour representation.

These occur because the **steps in colour gradation** used by high colour (15/16-bit) are not identical to that of true colour (24-bit). On systems capable of displaying 24-bit colour depth, Web-safe colours cease to be of any importance.

| FFFFFF | FFFF66 | FFFF33 | FFFF00 | CCFF66 | 66FFFF | 66FF33 | 66FF00 | 33FFFF | 33FFCC | 33FF66 | 33FF33 | 00FFFF | 00FFCC | 00FF66 | 00FF00 | FF00FF | FF0033 | FF0000 | 0000FF | 000033 | 000000 |

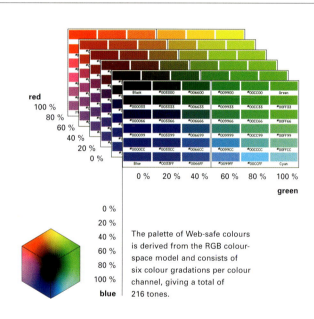

red
100 %
80 %
60 %
40 %
20 %
0 %

0 %   20 %   40 %   60 %   80 %   100 %

green

0 %
20 %
40 %
60 %
80 %
100 %

blue

The palette of Web-safe colours is derived from the RGB colour-space model and consists of six colour gradations per colour channel, giving a total of 216 tones.

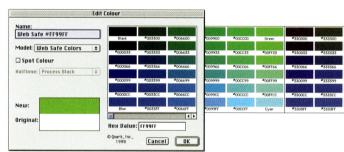

Quark XPress 5

Using 5 bits per colour channel results in different steps of colour gradation than would arise from using 8 bits per channel because the two numerical systems are not divisible by exactly the same factor. This leads to inconsistencies in representation.

Most colour-selection tools arrange this palette according to their hexadecimal code. This limits our working knowledge of the underlying colour model and because it does not group according to colour families also hinders our ability to make qualified choices.

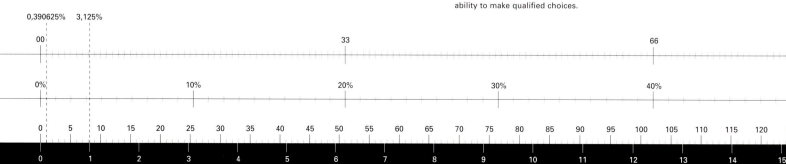

*"One of the givens of Web design, the holiest of holy truths, is the sanctity of the 216 Web-safe colour palette.
It's a rite of initiation for every Web designer or developer: use only these colours, we are told, and don't question why."*

David Lehn, Hadley Stern

Adobe GoLive

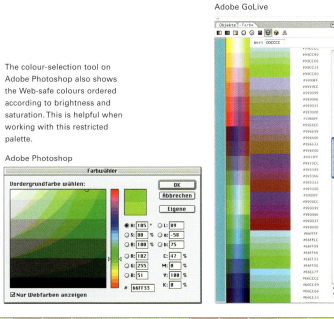

The colour-selection tool on
Adobe Photoshop also shows
the Web-safe colours ordered
according to brightness and
saturation. This is helpful when
working with this restricted
palette.

Adobe Photoshop

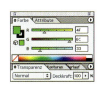

Macromedia Flash 5          Adobe Illustrator 10     Macromedia Freehand 9          Mac OS X                   Mac OS 9.2

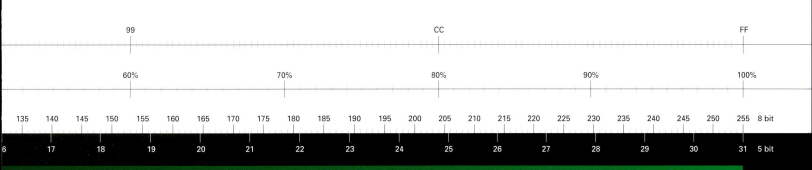

*"The real danger is not that computers will begin to think like men, but that men will begin to think like computers."*

Sydney J. Harris

Hexadecimal system

8-bit system

Translation of colour into code for the Internet is best
done using a hexadecimal system. Using this notation,
it is possible to express not only the Web-safe
colours, but also all the RGB tones.

## Working with colours

It is advisable to select all the colours using the same model so as to avoid possible inconsistencies in colour between the various design elements.

There is neither a standardised colour model nor are there any guidelines for how best to convert from one model to another. Because of this, values either get rounded up or down with each change causing inconsistencies to build up. This leads to the end result differing slightly – yet by comparison, visibly – from the original colour. A model offered by most programs is RGB. It follows, then, that when compiling layouts in which elements from several design programs are brought together, this colour model should be used.

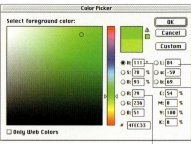

Adobe Photoshop 7

Within the RGB models the notation may change – an RGB value can thus be expressed on a scale between 0 and 255, as a percentage or in the hexadecimal system.

Macromedia Flash MX

 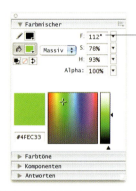

The program Flash MX. The values of this system suggest that it functions on the HSV model. An HLS model is used as a visual aid.

Mac OS X

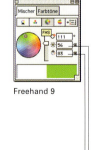

Freehand 9

The HLS system exists in several different varieties meaning that values in a sequence can get mixed up.

Adobe Photoshop 7

Program Director 8.5. Many programs offer a pre-selected palette; for a professional colour concept however, always switch over to a full range colour picker.

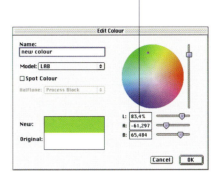

Adobe InDesign 2

Even the LAB model is not insusceptible to conversion shift.

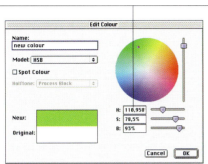

QuarkXPress 5

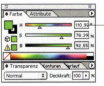

Switching between colour models causes shifts in tone due to repeatedly rounding up or down.

Adobe Illustrator 10

Macromedia Flash 5

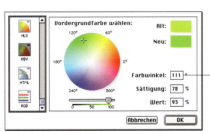

Mac OS 9.2

Mac OS X

Apple colour-selection application Crayons: the name of this colour-selection application evokes the use of physical materials. It is suitable for private use and entertainment purposes.

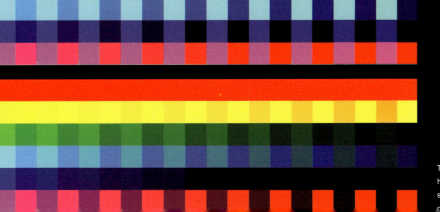

The two sequences shown here illustrate the gradual shift in colour tone caused by conversions.

## Why colours look different on the PC and Macintosh

The reproduction from data of colour, brightness and contrast varies greatly according to the platform – the two most common on the net being PCs and Macs. This is attributable to differences in **gamma settings** between the two systems.

The platform used as output is the determining factor – either the presentation is too whitewashed (Mac) or too dark (PC).

A video card functions using a voltage of between 0 and 5 volts. If the video card sends out no signal, i.e. 0 volts, black is displayed; 5 volts corresponds to white. There is not, however, a linear relationship between the voltage produced and the brightness on the screen. Hence, if a 2.5 volt signal is received, the image on the screen is not at 50% brightness, but instead somewhat darker, perhaps at around 25% brightness. This is accounted for in software packages by something known as gamma correction. The signals are adjusted while still in the computer to compensate for any misinterpretation by the monitor.

In carrying out this task, operating systems work from the premise that an 'average' monitor is being used. Unfortunately the exact gamma value of an 'average' monitor is not quite so easy to determine and estimates vary widely.

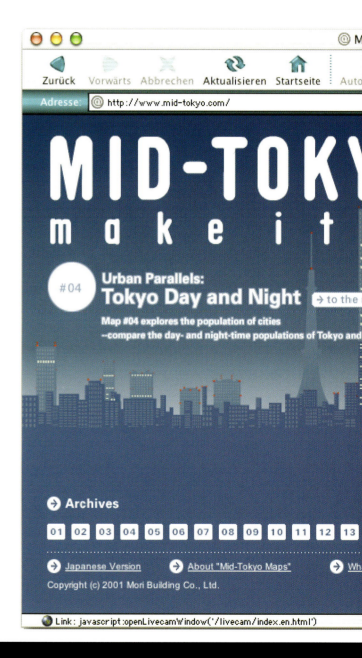

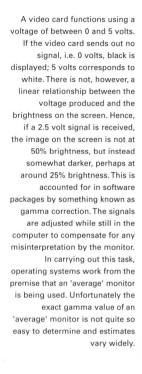

The **Mac OS** operating system uses a gamma value of 1.8.

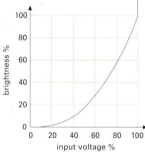

File contains a smooth gradient.

This is how it would look on the screen without gamma correction.

Gamma correction compensates for the non-linear increase in brightness.

The gradient appears smooth again.

Data processed using a Macintosh appears darker and richer in contrast if viewed on a PC.

The **Windows** operating system usually uses a gamma value of 2.2.

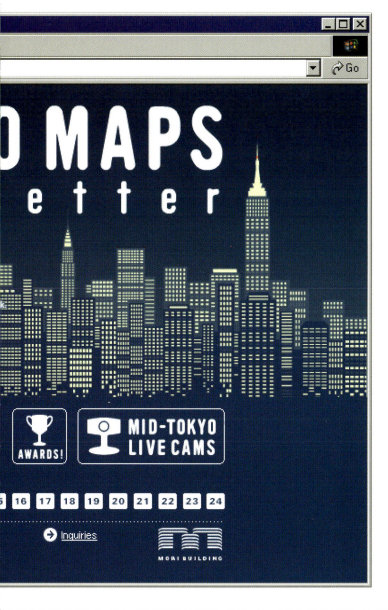

www.lessrain.de

Mac    PC

Even with data formats allowing the inclusion of gamma information, there are simply no reliable standards for the Web. Ideally, one is best off testing colour and brightness suitability on the platforms used by the target audience. More up-to-date graphics programs give the user a preview option that simulates the end result as it would be seen on other platforms.

Data processed using a PC appears lacklustre on the Mac platform, i.e. increased brightness, reduced contrast.

# The Media of Colour

1 2 3 4 **5** 6 7 8 9

There is more to colour than meets the eye. Everyone knows this from having seen how a photograph reveals discrepancies between the captured and "actual" colours or how a printed version of a document differs widely from the version represented on the screen. This chapter looks at the way colour representation varies, seen on different media.

## Differing representation on the screen and on paper

Colour is always influenced by the material or medium of transmission. In the physical world, it is the combined factors of reflection, remission and transmission that determine the colours of various materials. A quick comparison of material- and light-based colours is enough to demonstrate clearly that, because the means of production are so dissimilar, it is only possible to create a rough approximation.

see also pages 48|49

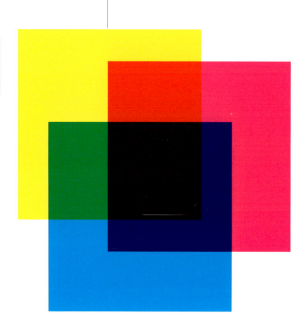

In the **subtractive system of colour mixture**, the primary colours cyan, magenta and yellow are used. Mixing all the colours together results in black. Lighter colours than those that make up the primary colours cannot be mixed without altering the saturation.

**CMYK**
For reasons of efficiency and precision a solid black as the fourth colour is used in offset printing.

Printing processes generally work using visual colour mixture i.e. the primary colours are printed next to each other, only combining to produce the various colour tones upon hitting the retina of the eye.

Pigment-based colours, whether process or solid colour, paint or textile colour are difficult to evaluate on the screen. There are, therefore, several colour systems offering printed colour samples as guides to orientation. The area of application determines which of the various colour models is used as the basis.

| C 50 | C 50 | C 0 |
| M 20 | M 50 | M 0 |
| Y 80 | Y 50 | Y 0 |
| K 0 | K 50 | K 80 |

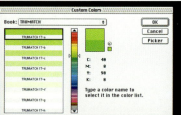

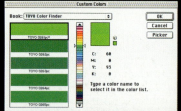

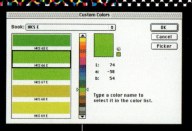

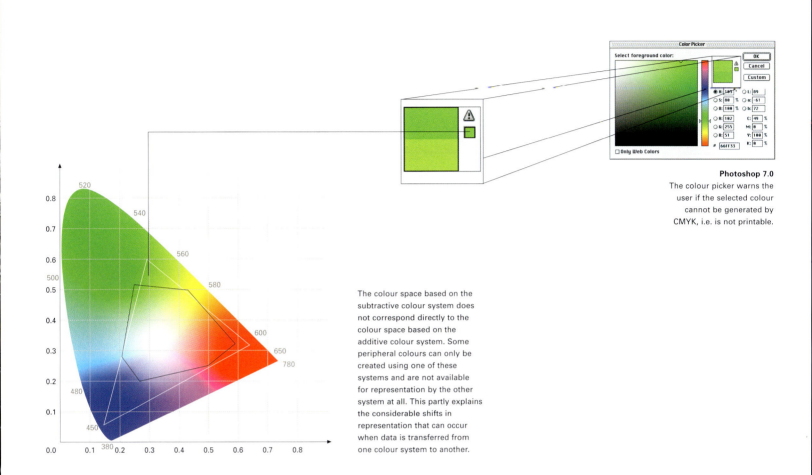

**Photoshop 7.0**
The colour picker warns the user if the selected colour cannot be generated by CMYK, i.e. is not printable.

The colour space based on the subtractive colour system does not correspond directly to the colour space based on the additive colour system. Some peripheral colours can only be created using one of these systems and are not available for representation by the other system at all. This partly explains the considerable shifts in representation that can occur when data is transferred from one colour system to another.

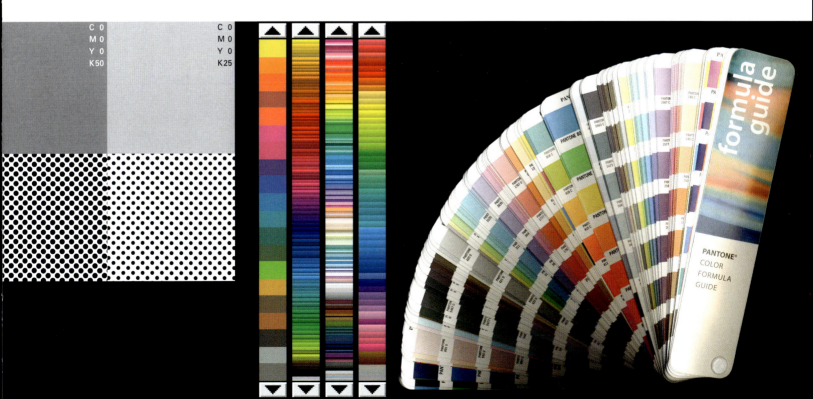

# Working with colour

The problem of colour inconsistencies between numerically identical colours in different programs is a headache, but still requires our attention. If various photo- or graphics-based elements are combined in one layout, there may well be noticeable discrepancies in the representation. This is sometimes down to the poor quality offered when previewing imported images and can have a negative effect on the overall impression of a layout. Because, after repeatedly **rounding** figures up or down, colour shifts can occur at a later stage in the browser, it is advisable to create graphic elements of the same type using the same program.

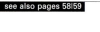
see also pages 58|59

Switching from RGB to CMYK (or vice-versa) tends to cause the most inconsistencies since the two colour models are not congruent. In practical terms, this means that, where possible, it is best to do all the work using the colour model that will be used by the output medium. Where a one-off conversion really is unavoidable, all data should be converted in the same stage of the design process.

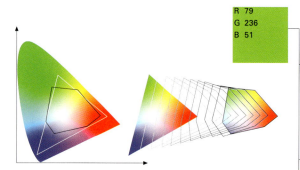

R 79
G 236
B 51

Colour management systems offer four different ways to map colours:

**Perceptual:** compresses the total gamut from one device's colour space into the gamut of another device's colour space. This preserves the visual relationship between colours by shifting all colours.

**Saturation:** reproduces the original image colour saturation when converting into the target device's colour space.

**Relative colourimetric:** when a colour in the current colour space is out of the gamut of the target colour space, it is mapped to the closest possible colour within the gamut, while colours that are in gamut are not affected.

**Absolute colourimetric:** colours match exactly with no adjustment made for white point or black point that would alter the image's brightness.

|  | QuarkXPress 5 | InDesign 2.0 | Illustrator 10 | Freehand 9 | Flash 5 eps | Director 8.5 | Photoshop 7 |
|---|---|---|---|---|---|---|---|

Original colour R=79, G=236, B=51 converted using CMYK

Screen representation in QuarkXPress

PDF file with RGB profile

PDF file with CMYK profile

When creating a PDF file using RGB- or CMYK-based conversion, colour values can shift to differing extents depending on which program is used to represent the colour at the output stage.

Colour management systems are intended to help ensure colour consistency across a range of different media. The idea is to coordinate as closely as possible the colour space used by input devices, e.g. scanners and digital cameras, with the colour space of the screen and, above all, with that of the output device, e.g. the printer.
Colour profiles are mainly used in printing, the stage of production offering the narrowest colour space.

Colour profiles offering standardised colour representation for the screen have yet to take off due to the broad range of output systems in use.

"Experience is simply the name we give our mistakes."
Oscar Wilde

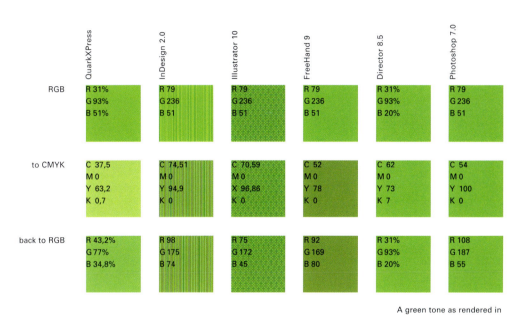

| | QuarkXPress | InDesign 2.0 | Illustrator 10 | FreeHand 9 | Director 8.5 | Photoshop 7.0 |
|---|---|---|---|---|---|---|
| RGB | R 31% G 93% B 51% | R 79 G 236 B 51 | R 79 G 236 B 51 | R 79 G 236 B 51 | R 31% G 93% B 20% | R 79 G 236 B 51 |
| to CMYK | C 37,5 M 0 Y 63,2 K 0,7 | C 74,51 M 0 Y 94,9 K 0 | C 70,59 M 0 X 96,86 K 0 | C 52 M 0 Y 78 K 0 | C 62 M 0 Y 73 K 7 | C 54 M 0 Y 100 K 0 |
| back to RGB | R 43,2% G 77% B 34,8% | R 98 G 175 B 74 | R 75 G 172 B 45 | R 92 G 169 B 80 | R 31% G 93% B 20% | R 108 G 187 B 55 |

A green tone as rendered in a range of programs using RGB settings then converted to CMYK mode and once more back to RGB.

**Left colour swatches:**

C 55 / M 0 / Y 97 / K 0
C 60 / M 0 / Y 100 / K 0
C 54 / M 0 / Y 100 / K 0
C 49 / M 0 / Y 82 / K 0

**CMYK mode**

| C 100 M 0 Y 0 K 0 | C 0 M 100 Y 0 K 0 | C 0 M 0 Y 100 K 0 | C 0 M 100 Y 100 K 0 | C 100 M 0 Y 100 K 0 | C 100 M 100 Y 0 K 0 |
|---|---|---|---|---|---|
| R 0 G 255 B 255 | R 255 G 0 B 255 | R 255 G 255 B 0 | R 255 G 0 B 0 | R 0 G 255 B 0 | R 0 G 0 B 255 |
| C 49 M 0 Y 11 K 0 | C 26 M 75 Y 0 K 0 | C 7 M 0 Y 100 K 0 | C 0 M 95 Y 100 K 0 | C 62 M 0 Y 100 K 0 | C 85 M 74 Y 0 K 0 |

Colours rendered at full-saturation in RGB mode are no longer fully saturated when converted to CMYK mode.

Colour management systems simulate colour results as produced by a particular method of printing. Hence various representations of green are created for the screen while the tone remains unchanged numerically. The profile information is given in the form of a tag attached to the data and can be altered or reset at any time.

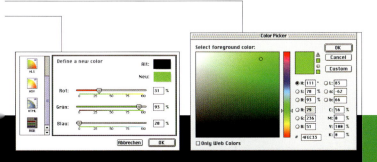

ColourSync CMYK-profile
Euroscale coated CMYK-profile
Euroscale uncoated CMYK-profile
Japan standard CMYK-profile
U.S. sheetfed coated CMYK-profile
U.S. sheetfed uncoated CMYK-profile
U.S. web coated CMYK-profile
U.S. web uncoated CMYK-profile

**Crossmedial colour application**

When designing communication concepts, the colour concept used should remain viable across a range of media. To this end, it helps to be able to fix the colour to be used as solid colour in, say, Pantone, that to be used as process colour in CMYK and that for the screen in Hex or RGB.

Still the traditional medium of paper is given the most attention to ensuring that it lays down the corporate identity, which the screen will eventually reflect. This explains the widespread use of white backgrounds on the screen.

Communication concepts are increasingly being planned as a package for use across a variety of media. The resulting concepts view each medium as equally valid, sometimes even taking the idiosyncrasies of the screen into account when designing for paper.

In recent years, there has also been a tendency for company logos to be stripped of their original house colours and henceforth appear only occasionally in colour format. The **company logo** is then applied in positive or negative rather than colour and likely to be rendered over a picture as a semi-transparent overlay. This has a lot to do with the fact that the technology necessary for superimposing text over pictures has already been available to designers for some time; it is only recently that it has started to take off.

www.nike.com

**www.wilkhahn.de**
Corporate identity concept for the firm Wilkhahn. The same colour scheme, with each colour component appearing in similar quantities, is used in print and screen formats.

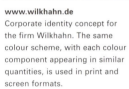

Solis F. High Tech mit high Touch.

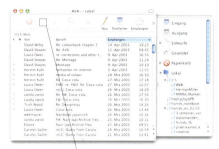

Apple's product and communication concept. The device itself and the software installed on it are tied together, in terms of colour and "feel", by a continual design theme. There is a seemless meeting of physical and virtual worlds.

Software

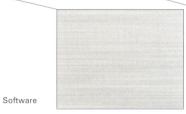
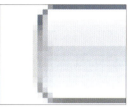

Hardware

The corporate identity concept for Expo 2000 represents a direct transfer of the characteristics of computer-based media into print format – the logo is flexible and can also be used in combination with a wide variety of colours.

**Colour in representations**

see also pages 64|65

The quality of **colour matching** plays a vital role in the lifelike representation of objects. Which colours are used depends primarily on the context, yet – where photographs are concerned – also on the quality of the picture. In e-commerce, a white or neutral grey context tends to be used to keep the effect as natural-looking as possible. A glance at the more **amateur end** of the Internet market exposes the difficulties involved in getting digital colours to look natural.

www.nike.com/nikegoddess

www.ebay.de

www.yoox.com

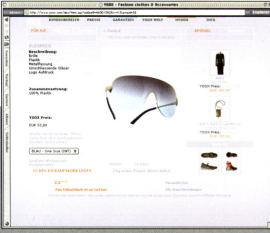

**www.ebay.de**
Photographic representation of the Apple Powerbook G4 and the Power Mac G4: provided the viewer is familiar with the object in question, he or she should be able to recognise it despite the understated colours.

"Pictures must not be too picturesque."
Ralph Waldo Emerson

www.apple.com

**www.volkswagen.de**
Using the configurator feature, the user is able to design a personalised car – here "cedar green" has been selected.

**www.mobile.de**
The used-car market on the Internet – here are representations of the same model in the same colour "cedar green".

## Cross-medial inspiration

As a new medium becomes increasingly widespread, there is, at the same time, reflection on the medium it is replacing. The characteristics of paper – its physical quality, its transitoriness, and the direct nature of interaction – seem to have become a source of inspiration for website design, as well as refining already familiar navigational methods such as the turning of pages and textured colour variations that, when photographed, still manage to exhibit a sensuality charged with life.

www.copyrightdavis.com

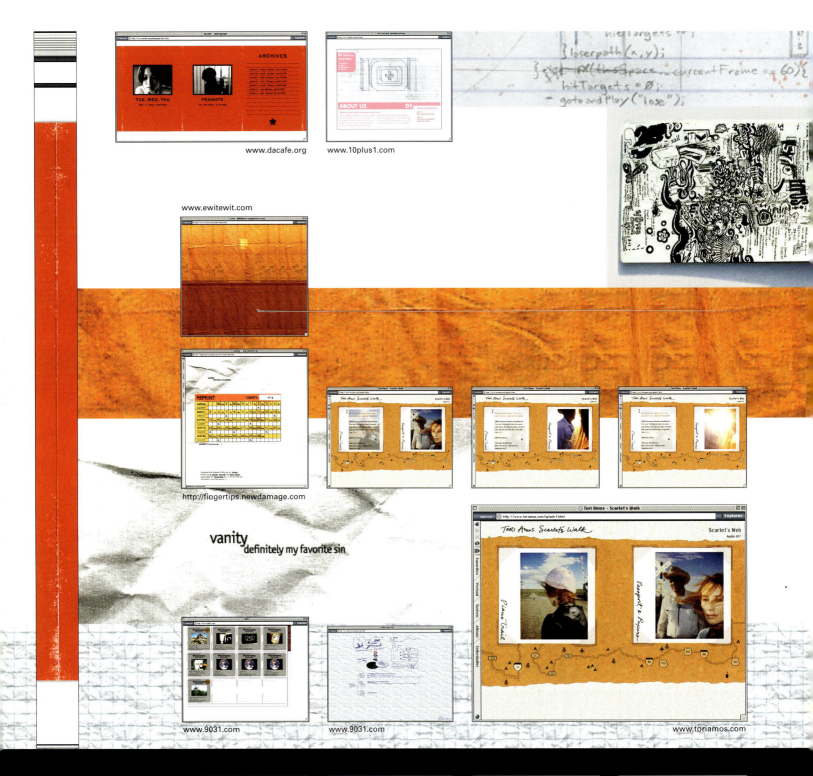

www.dacafe.org

www.10plus1.com

www.ewitewit.com

http://fingertips.newdamage.com

vanity definitely my favorite sin

www.9031.com

www.9031.com

www.toriamos.com

"Really we create nothing. We merely plagiarize nature."

Jean Baitaillon

www.nikewoman.com

"One touch of nature makes the whole world kin."  William Shakespeare

www.quinta-feira.org

www.imustcreate.com

www.lunapod.com

www.dinnickandhowells.com

u really know where you're going? do you have a
of-action to take the kinks out of your road to the
e?.. you can reach and find happiness. you can
for that plain peace-of-mind which you desire
ou have to do is turn the key and open the
www.liquidcat.com  door.

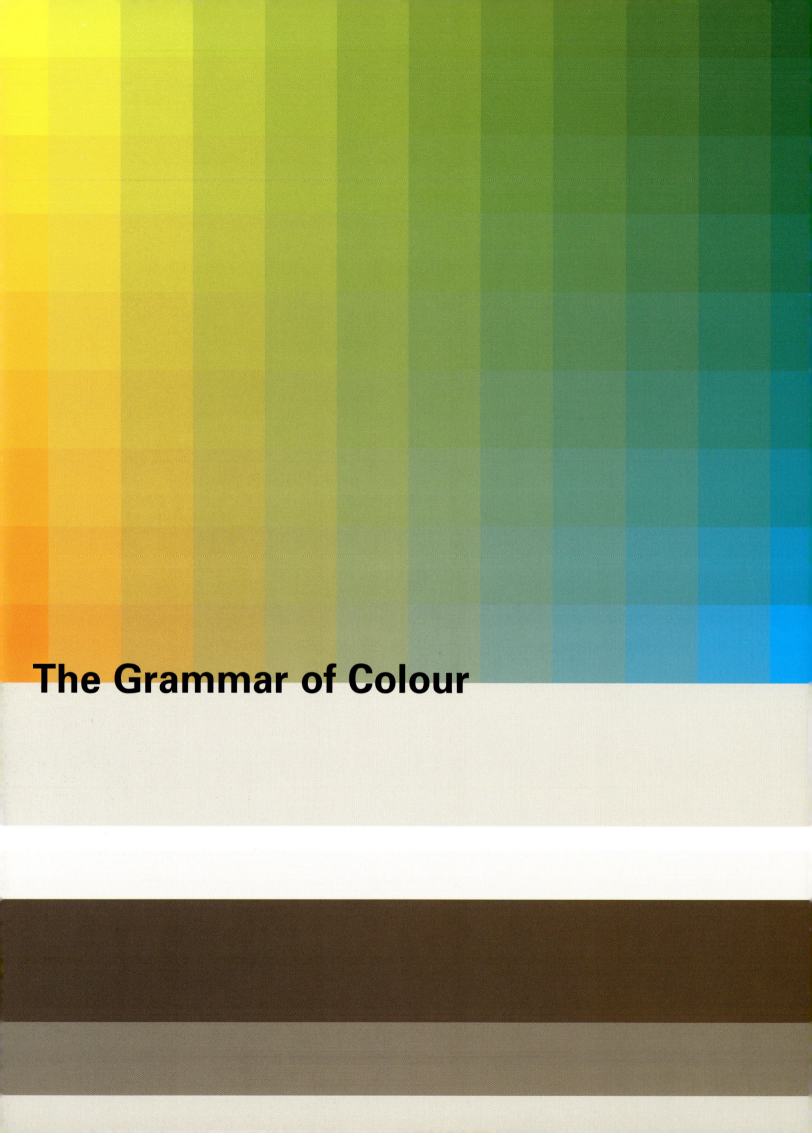

# The Grammar of Colour

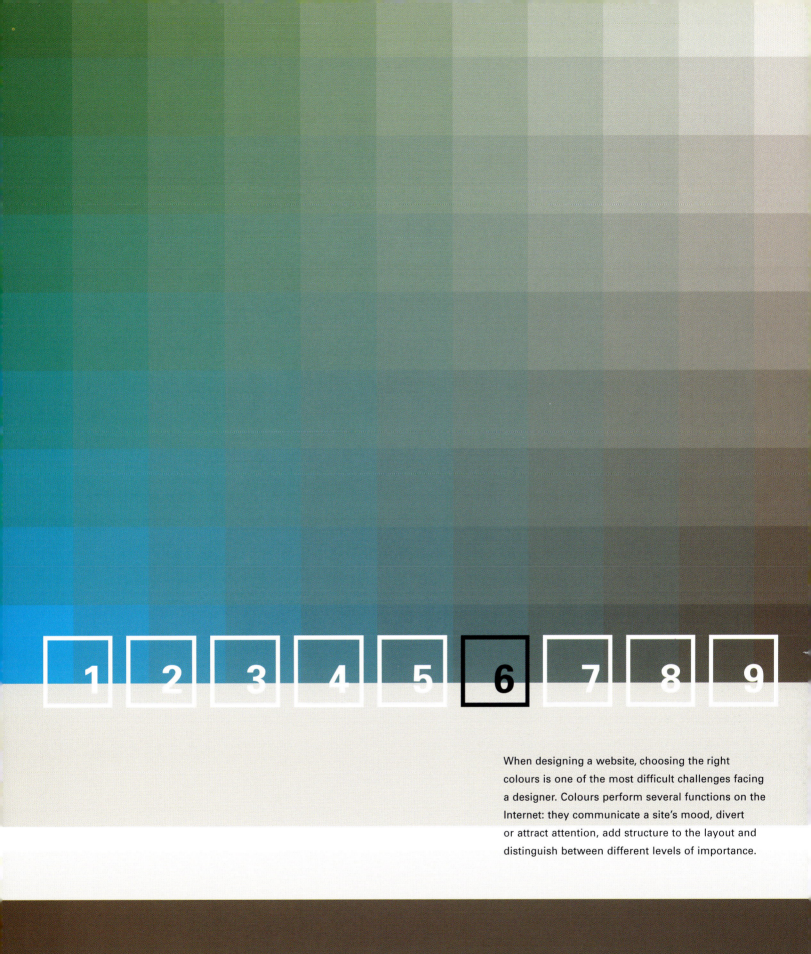

When designing a website, choosing the right colours is one of the most difficult challenges facing a designer. Colours perform several functions on the Internet: they communicate a site's mood, divert or attract attention, add structure to the layout and distinguish between different levels of importance.

**Colour contrasts usually don't appear separate**

In theory, when designing for digital applications, the same basic rules of more classical forms such as print media also apply.

One significant difference is that using colour on the screen does not increase the cost. In contrast to printed media, colour may be used as lavishly as one wants.

While the limitations are few, it is worth bearing in mind that a screen-based medium where the display emits light will tend to intensify the effect of colour contrasts. The added dimension of time and the possibilities of interaction broaden the options of a designer.

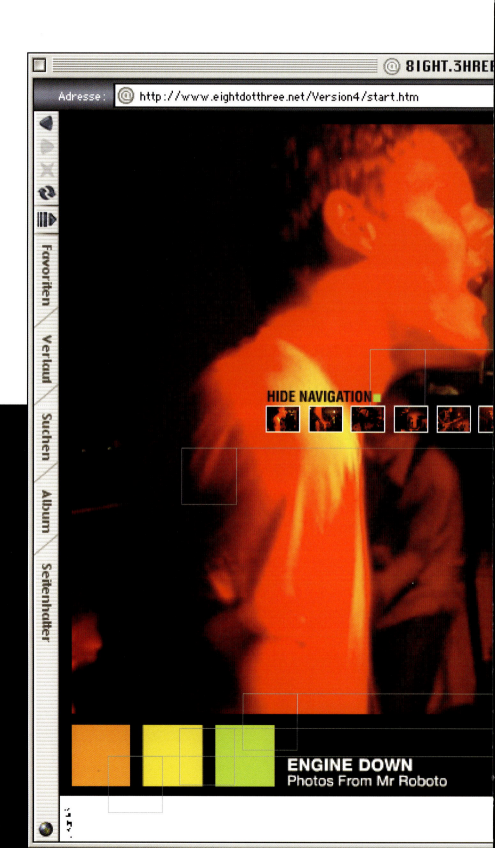

Theoretically speaking it is possible to identify eight
different colour contrasts; in practice, however, most
colour contrasts appear in combination. The challenge
facing the designer is how best to make creative use
of them and communicate the content in a way that is
both clear and attractive.

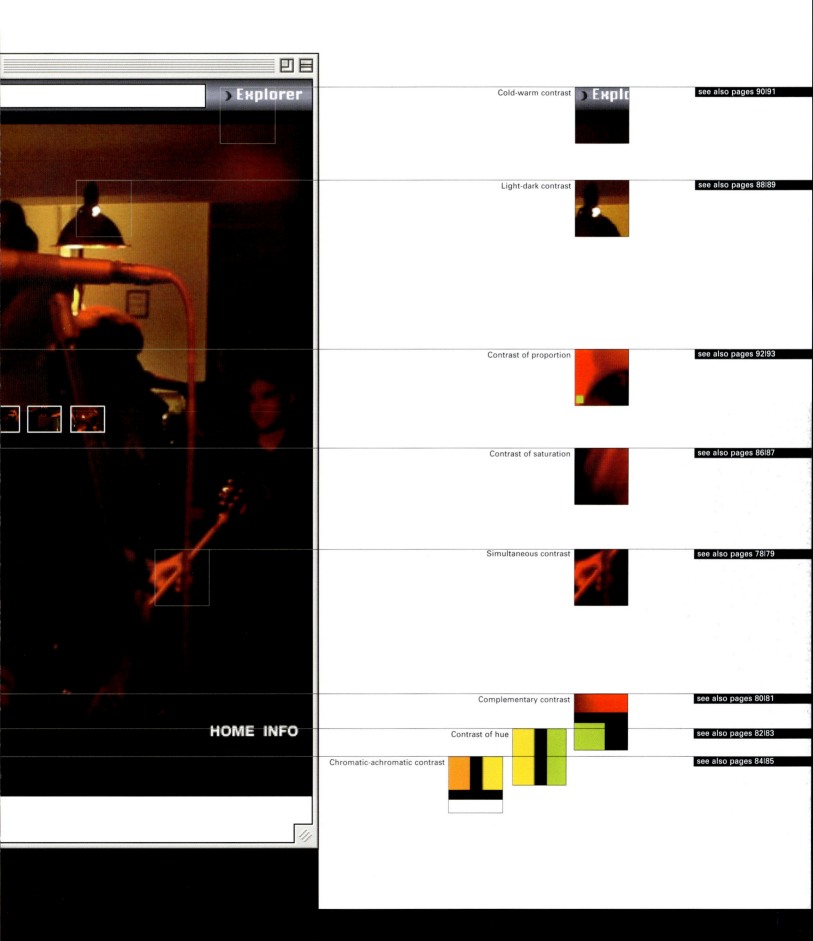

Explorer

Cold-warm contrast     see also pages 90|91

Light-dark contrast     see also pages 88|89

Contrast of proportion     see also pages 92|93

Contrast of saturation     see also pages 86|87

Simultaneous contrast     see also pages 78|79

Complementary contrast     see also pages 80|81

Contrast of hue     see also pages 82|83

Chromatic-achromatic contrast     see also pages 84|85

HOME INFO

## Simultaneous contrast

It is impossible to avoid simultaneous contrasts. Due to the lack of "absolute" **colour memory** we perceive all colours relative to their context – this is all the more true of screen-based media.

The context influences the overall impression and a shift in colour value results. The reasons for this shift can be traced back to the human eye's tendency to reinforce contrasts.

The colour used as **desktop background** on a website is enough to make a significant difference to the overall effect of it. When weighing up which colours to use for the site, it is a good idea to take a monochrome, achromatic theme set at medium brightness for your computer's desktop. This is visually unobtrusive and enables comparisons of brightness, contrast and effect to be made against as neutral a background as possible.

see also pages 26|27

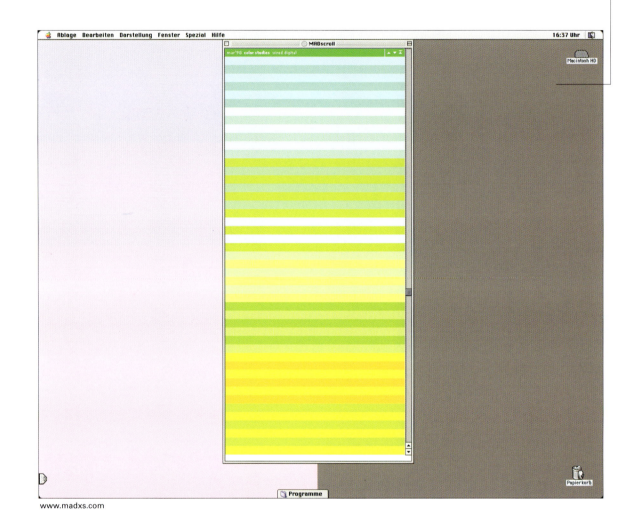

www.madxs.com

By varying the background, the monochrome strips of colour are made to appear lighter at some points and darker at others.

Stimulation of only one type of cone by a highly saturated colour causes after images in complementary colours. When deciding which colours to use for a website, it is advisable to ensure that reading-intensive areas of the site require similar levels of processing by the visual apparatus. Large areas containing extensive quantities of text should be rendered in low-saturation colours.

Chromatic-achromatic shift

Light-dark shift

Colour value shift

Shift may occur where layout elements of the same colour are positioned on areas of different colours. The effect of a simultaneous contrast depends on the size and positioning of an element.

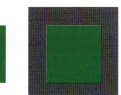 

**www.bubble.be**
Used well, simultaneous contrasts can be effective on the screen: this animation continually changes the colours producing dynamic colour shifts. The eye of the viewer permanently has to work at the very limit of its adaptive capabilities.

   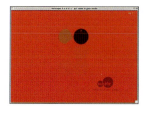

 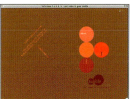 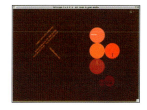 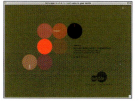

Seen against the changing background, the colour strip, which is in fact monochrome, appears to undergo a shift: the left end appears lighter than the right.

## Complementary contrast

Complementary contrast is the best-known type of contrast by far. The term describes the apparent intensification of a colour when combined with its complementary opposite i.e. the colour lying directly across from it on the colour wheel. Due to differences in the way colour wheels are arranged, colours taken as complementary pairs do vary from wheel to wheel.

While the combination of high-saturation colours comes across as too loud, combinations of lower-saturation complementary colours form a robust basis for a classic-looking design. Used in conjunction with a **contrast of proportion**, it is possible to achieve eye-catching effects on elements such as navigation pointers using complementary colours.

see also pages 34|35

www.aveda.com

www.volumeone.com

Because red-green colour blindness is the most common form of visual impediment, it is often a good idea to include a further contrasting factor such as brightness.

www.phojekt.com

www.mariolalich.com

www.smartmoney.com

The medium also offers the possibility of leaving the choice of colour up to the user.

www.flong.com

www.renvall.se

www.hurenaanzee.be

www.breathnaigh.com

www.123klan.com

www.treelogic.com

"There is no blue without yellow and without orange."
Vincent van Gogh

see also pages 92|93

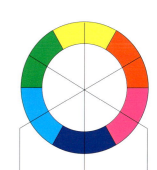

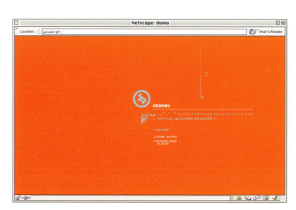

www.doma.tv

www.imgsrc.co

www.weareshit.com

www.spakkamo.org

www.smartmoney.com

www.415.com

www.axe.nl

The asymmetrical weighting of saturation within a complementary contrast means a low-saturation tone from one colour family is used in combination with a high-saturation tone taken

## The contrast of hue

The contrast of hue describes the vivid combination of several colours of equal saturation. This colourful type of palette is often associated with childhood, fun and playfulness. This also embraces the tints otherwise known as pastels. Less brashly coloured harmonies result if the **saturation is reduced**.

Whether something is seen as "colourful" or not depends on several factors. Besides cultural background, tradition and the various **meanings** associated with colours, context plays a deciding role in determining what comes across as too colourful.

Even from a distance, colourful material addresses its target groups: children, youth and fun.

www.hitentertainment.com

www.kika.de

www.southparkmovie.com

www.disney.de

see also pages 28|29

"Our flag is red, white and blue, but our nation is a rainbow – red, yellow, brown, black and white -- and we're all precious in God's sight."
Jesse Jackson

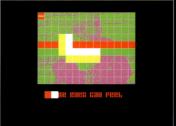

www.shapesquad.com

see also pages 120|121

By repositioning the blocks of colour so their edges no longer touch, a chromatic-achromatic contrast can be generated – large areas of white reduce the impression of colourfulness due to the excessive brightness produced by the white area of the screen.

see also pages 84|85

Conversely, adding black to the layout further energises the contrast.

www.anatomico.cl

www.joeboxer.com

www.24hr.se

http://.absolut.com

www.oneaftertheother.com

www.mks.jp.org

www.vitra.com

www.copyrightdavis.com

www.816babi.com

www.owenlogik.com

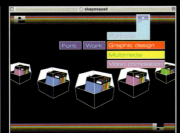

## Chromatic-achromatic contrast

Chromatic-achromatic contrast describes the effect of using gradations from the grey palette – or very pale gradations of other colours – in combination with high-saturation colours. If used together with a **contrast of proportion**, this forms a solid basis for a screen design. Reading comfort is increased if large areas of the screen are either rendered in low-saturation or not saturated at all. Navigational and interactive elements such as menu choices or links on the other hand are best emphasised in high-saturation colour. The neutral backdrop amplifies the effect of fully saturated elements.

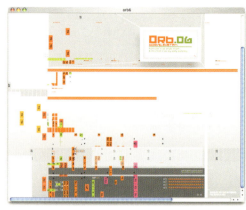

**www.apple.com**
An achromatic monochrome backdrop keeps the true impression of a colour intact and is therefore a firm favourite for use in product presentation as the colours seem to leap off the screen.

www.orangebleu.net

"I don't want any colour to be noticeable. I don't want it to operate in the modernist sense as colour, something independent… Full, saturated colours have an emotional significance I want to avoid."

Lucian Freud

**www.aamertaher.com**
A monochromatic medium-grey backdrop dampens colour. Bright colours rendered against this theme lack energy.

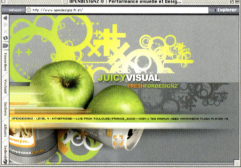

www.opendesignz.fr.st

**www.superlooper.com**
Weighting the colour ratio in favour of the high-saturation colour evokes the effect of simultaneous contrast – the neutral colour appears tinted.

**www.stoav.be**
Chromatic-achromatic contrasts are reinforced if the tones also vary in intrinsic brightness.

**www.zitrones.com**
Despite high levels of intrinsic brightness, a light chromatic colour lends itself well to use as a mode of emphasis against a light achromatic background – the contrast is understated yet it works.

see also pages 92|93

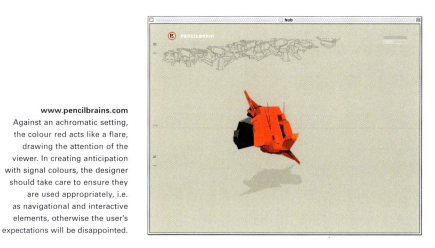

**www.pencilbrains.com**
Against an achromatic setting, the colour red acts like a flare, drawing the attention of the viewer. In creating anticipation with signal colours, the designer should take care to ensure they are used appropriately, i.e. as navigational and interactive elements, otherwise the user's expectations will be disappointed.

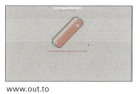 

www.out.to

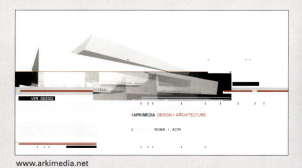

www.arkimedia.net

www.arkimedia.net

www.arkimedia.net

## The contrast of saturation

The term "contrast of saturation" refers to the combination of different tonal gradations taken from the same colour family. This kind of variation in tone produces a balanced, solid-looking theme. Effects of texture and depth may be added by altering the levels of brightness helping to structure a layout and classify information according to importance.

It is nevertheless advisable to use another colour to pick out any navigational elements – this ensures they remain distinct. When using qualitative contrast, there is the danger of a carefully balanced theme simply coming across as boring.

The screen offers the possibility of using subtle modulation to alter the interplay of colours during viewing thereby holding the user's attention.

www.paulkellydesign.com

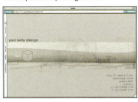    

"I like boring things."  Andy Warhol

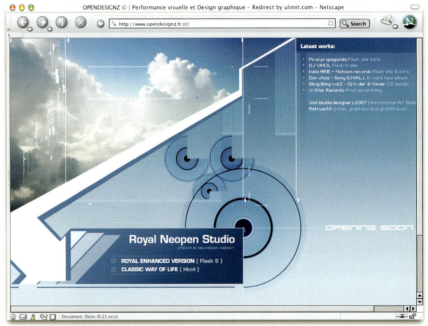

www.opendesignz.fr.st

www.adcny.org

www.coral.de

    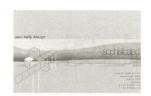

www.innerblitz.com

www.jeupinc.com

www.burntgraphix.com

**www.milla.de**
Modulation in the tonal
value between two colour
families creates a slick-looking
alternation which charges the
layout with energy.

# The light-dark contrast

The light-dark contrast is the most important type of contrast for the screen. Time spent fine-tuning the contrast here pays off not only in terms of aesthetics, it is also an ergonomic necessity.

The light-based nature of the medium screen depends heavily on the lighting conditions of the environment and thus demands sufficient contrast. This is even more important since the contrasts vary in appearance depending on the output platform and the type of display unit. Achieving a subtle interplay of colour should remain the design objective.

see also pages 44|45

www.craigarmstrong.com

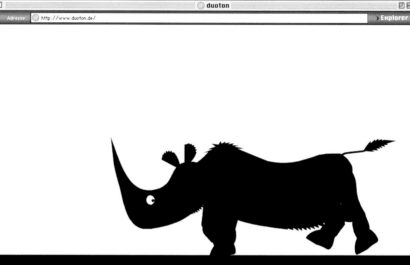

**www.duoton.de**
Sharp edges of contrast representing jumps in brightness of almost 100% put a strain on the eye if viewed for long periods of time. Particularly in bad lighting conditions, the glare may be uncomfortable for the viewer.

www.nungu.com

www.neleman.com

**www.angeloplessas.com**
With softer edges there is a gradual increase in brightness more typical of natural light.

If the contrasts are too harsh it can lead to overcast contours, flicker effects and visual illusions start to set in. With **text** in particular, consideration must be given to these factors.

see also pages 106|107

www.deutsch-guggenheim-berlin.de

www.breathnaigh.com

www.potatoland.org

www.guerillaone.com

Light dark contrast is also relevant to colour combinations. To get sufficient levels of contrast, a visible difference in brightness is required. If levels of intrinsic brightness do not vary sufficiently between the two colours, their brightness can be adjusted accordingly in order to get the desired contrast.

www.osborne.de

**www.constructionkid.nl**
Contrasts in brightness can be used to create an impression of texture and depth.

"Shadow is a colour as light is, but less brilliant; light and shadow are only the relation of two tones."

Paul Cézanne

## Cold-warm contrast

see also pages 44|45

The term cold-warm contrast describes the combination of a colour taken from a **warm position** on the colour wheel with a colour taken from a cold position. This contrast relies on a perceptive phenomenon which appears to cause cold colours to recede and warm colours to stand out. If these colours are implemented in a way that corresponds to these expectations, the illusion of depth is achieved.

A cold-warm contrast can also be created using neutral tones. Simultaneous and complementary contrasts tend to cause the grey palette to shift towards either cold or warm. Cold-warm contrast can also be created within **related colour families** and as such represents a sophisticated alternative to the contrast of saturation.

**www.bulthaup.de**
Seen here, the grey palette comes across as cool – it is therefore ideal for bringing out the warm natural tones in these photographs.

--> Logout
--> Übersicht

Shopping
Marktplatz & Auktionen
Best Price
Lottoservice
Reisen & Events
Motor & Sport
Lifestyle & Singles
Club Inter@ctive
Erotik
Kino & DVD
Handy Specials
News & Facts
Jobs & Karriere
Finanzen

**www.superlooper.de**
If arranged contrary to expectations so that the background is represented in a warm colour and the foreground in a cool colour, the result is a figure/ground illusion: the object is in the foreground one minute and in the background the next.

www.berlinale.de

www.pleatsplease.com

www.danpearlman.com

www.q-milk.de

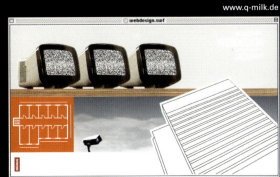

**The contrast of proportion**

Contrast of proportion refers to the proportional relationship between colours. Symmetrical distribution, i.e. different colours used in roughly equal amounts comes across as visually balanced, sometimes even dull. Altering the weight of the combination produces a more dramatic relationship.

Red is guaranteed to raise levels of attention but soon becomes tiring in large amounts.

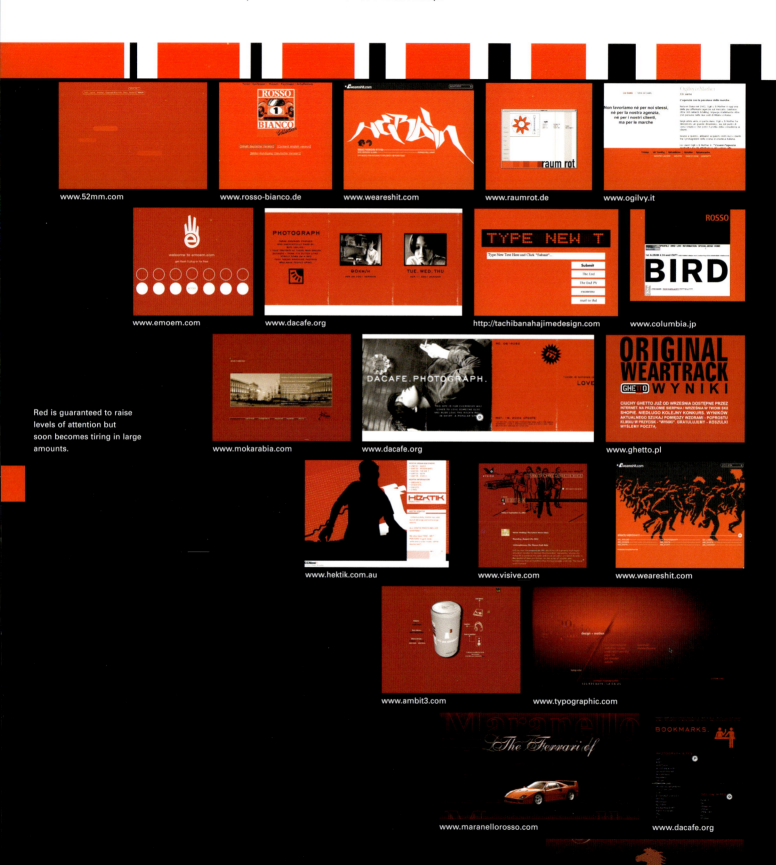

www.52mm.com

www.rosso-bianco.de

www.weareshit.com

www.raumrot.de

www.ogilvy.it

www.emoem.com

www.dacafe.org

http://tachibanahajimedesign.com

www.columbia.jp

www.mokarabia.com

www.dacafe.org

www.ghetto.pl

www.hektik.com.au

www.visive.com

www.weareshit.com

www.ambit3.com

www.typographic.com

www.maranellorosso.com

www.dacafe.org

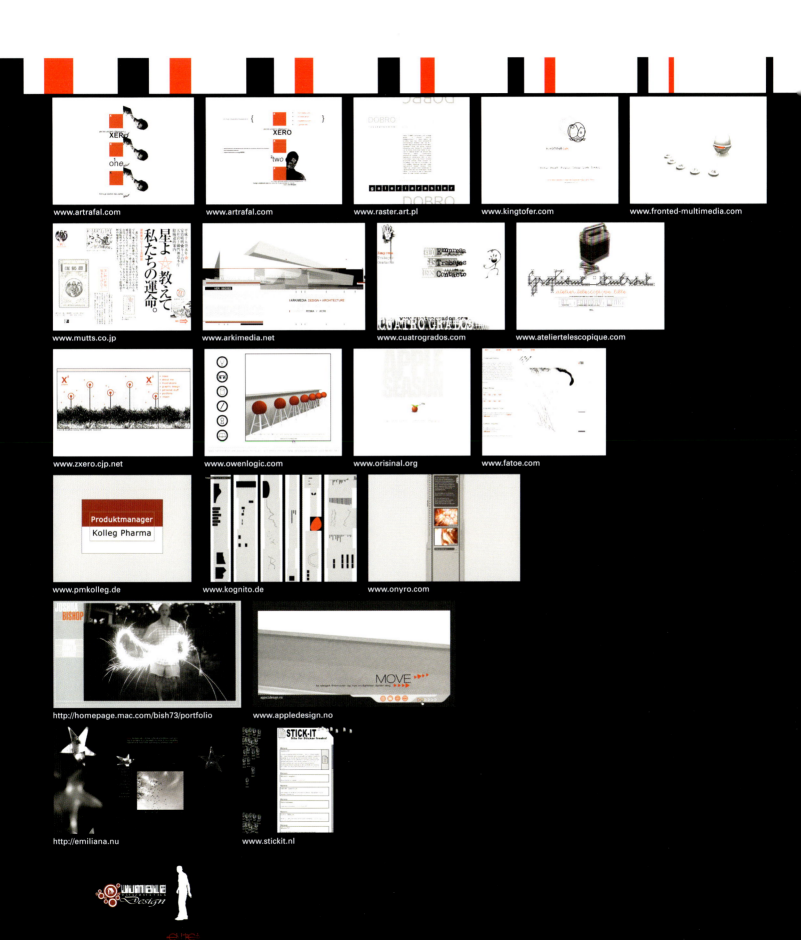

www.artrafal.com

www.artrafal.com

www.raster.art.pl

www.kingtofer.com

www.fronted-multimedia.com

www.mutts.co.jp

www.arkimedia.net

www.cuatrogrados.com

www.ateliertelescopique.com

www.zxero.cjp.net

www.owenlogic.com

www.orisinal.org

www.fatoe.com

www.pmkolleg.de

www.kognito.de

www.onyro.com

http://homepage.mac.com/bish73/portfolio

www.appledesign.no

http://emiliana.nu

www.stickit.nl

www.geocities.com/jumble_667

**The contrast of proportion**

The combination of chromatic and achromatic tones
is a particular favourite on the Internet.
Here, dynamically weighted quantitative contrasts
tend to work well – while the brightly coloured
tones make a nice initial impression, the proportion
of chromatic colour is then gradually reduced until
eventually only a minimal level is left as a mode
of **emphasis**.

**www.digit1.com**

Here, contrast of proportion is
used in conjunction with
chromatic-achromatic contrast to
display the status of navigational
elements.

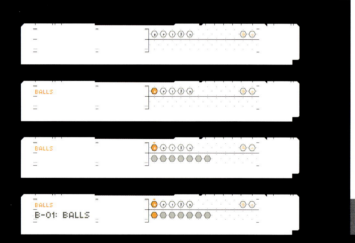

www.braun.de

www.seven.co.nz

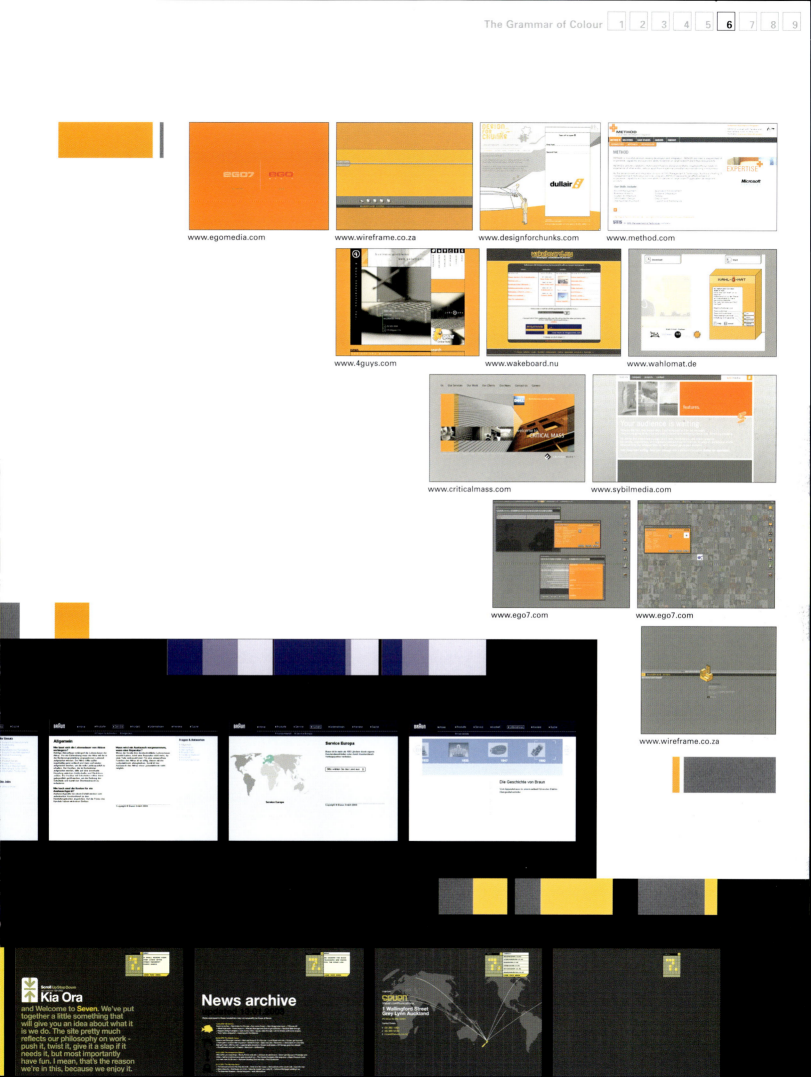

www.egomedia.com   www.wireframe.co.za   www.designforchunks.com   www.method.com

www.4guys.com   www.wakeboard.nu   www.wahlomat.de

www.criticalmass.com   www.sybilmedia.com

www.ego7.com   www.ego7.com

www.wireframe.co.za

# Texture and pattern

Texture and pattern rely on visual colour mixtures. While a pattern comprises clearly recognisable **blocks repeated** over and over again, texture does not appear to consist of obvious blocks. Pattern and texture have always been a means of creating rich and colourful effects and indeed continue to serve this purpose on the screen.

Texture provides an ideal way of structuring a layout so that the various zones are clearly defined, e.g. by making a distinction between interactive elements and information content.

They represent an alternative to solid blocks of colour. The texture itself should not, however, contain high levels of contrast as this may well detract from text or image content.

Variations in texture can be used in order to keep navigational sections of the screen distinct from the content areas.

http://elixir.blastradius.com

www.6um.com

www.crailtap.com

www.amnesia.com.br

www.chinaoverload.com

Apple Quick Time player

www.edenfx.com

www.magnetstudio.net

www.aniadesign.com

www.fork.de

www.burnfield.com

www.burnfield.com

www.burnfield.com

www.surfstation.lu

www.surfstation.lu

www.surfstation.lu

www.surfstation.lu

www.surfstation.lu

The use of lively patterns or textures based on real-life materials such as blotting paper, **wood** or brick are predominantly confined to the more amateur of Web pages where they nevertheless remain a firm favourite. Faster transmission rates enable the inclusion of generous amounts of graphics and pictures, an attractive way of livening up monotone screen space.

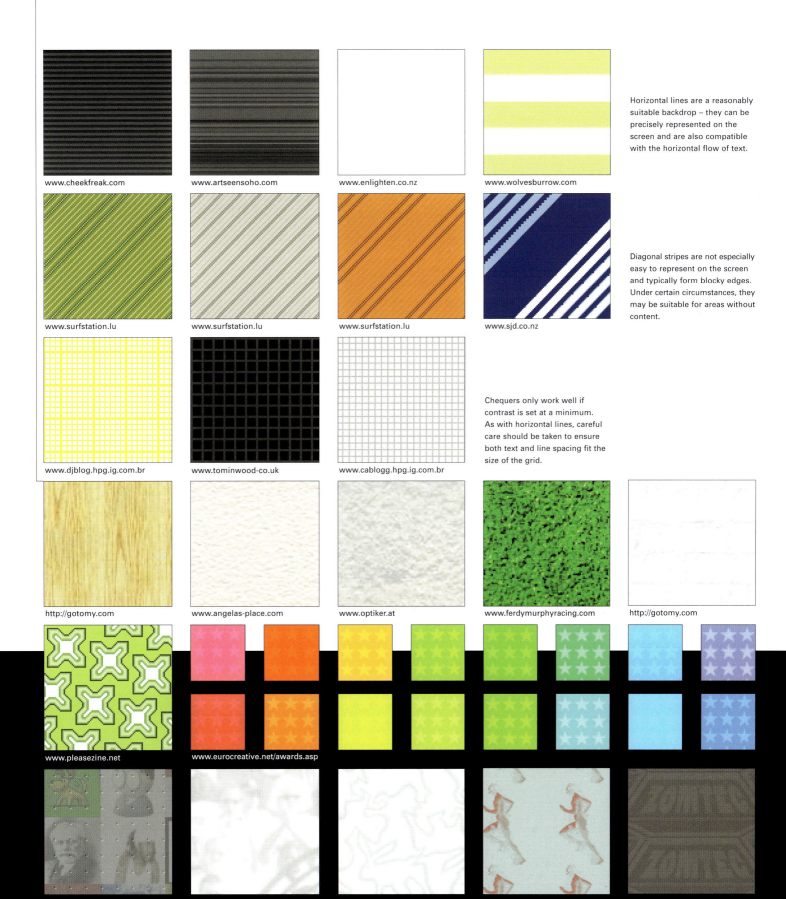

Horizontal lines are a reasonably suitable backdrop – they can be precisely represented on the screen and are also compatible with the horizontal flow of text.

Diagonal stripes are not especially easy to represent on the screen and typically form blocky edges. Under certain circumstances, they may be suitable for areas without content.

Chequers only work well if contrast is set at a minimum. As with horizontal lines, careful care should be taken to ensure both text and line spacing fit the size of the grid.

www.cheekfreak.com

www.artseensoho.com

www.enlighten.co.nz

www.wolvesburrow.com

www.surfstation.lu

www.surfstation.lu

www.surfstation.lu

www.sjd.co.nz

www.djblog.hpg.ig.com.br

www.tominwood-co.uk

www.cablogg.hpg.ig.com.br

http://gotomy.com

www.angelas-place.com

www.optiker.at

www.ferdymurphyracing.com

http://gotomy.com

www.pleasezine.net

www.eurocreative.net/awards.asp

## Colour gradations

Colour gradations are frowned upon by many designers. They can seem too dramatic if not incorporated in a subtle enough way, particularly where modulation spans two **colour families**. Apart from the aesthetic aspect, there are also ergonomic reasons why colour gradations should be avoided – in terms of contrast they cause the relationship between the foreground and background to fluctuate. This can significantly affect the **readability** of sections of text.

The almost imperceptible modulation of colour and brightness levels has nevertheless become an established design technique. It imitates the irregular play of natural light and helps to structure large areas of the screen.

www.vibes.net.au

Quicktime Player          Mac OS X Calculator

www.ihearithurts.com

www.moloko.co.uk

www.ala.ch

www.superlooper.de

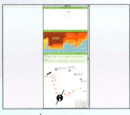

www.madxs.com

www.electronicmiracles.com

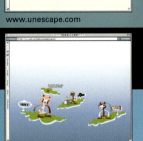

www.unescape.com

www.jotto.com

www.neocite.com

www.electronicmiracles.com

**PTC ProEngineer**
The work environment of this CAD software provides different shading options e.g. a colour gradation for the background. This gradation supports the three-dimensional impression of the rendered parts in the foreground.

see also pages 106|107

www.imustcreate.com

www.thehorusproject.com

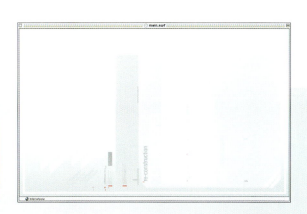

www.amoebalabs.com

www.freshthrills.com

www.ancientartz.com

www.derush.net

www.omniaband.com

www.urthgirl.com

www.muidlatif.cjb.net

www.amplified.nu

www.mindmeldcreative.com

www.newworldodour.com

## Colour and photography

Improved rates of transmission and screens with higher colour depth have made the incorporation of pictures both more viable and more attractive with websites increasingly imitating the visual formats of film or glossy magazines. The screen has become a window through which we can regard the world; text and characters are blended in, like through a camera's viewfinder.

Colour is typically used in subtle ways. In the photographic-cinematic field, this can be seen in the way motifs, viewing angles and focus are used together with time of day, lighting and filters. Seen through the lens of a camera, colour becomes a **complex** and animated phenomenon.

www.lessrain.de

www.lessrain.co.uk

www.bowieart.com

"When words become unclear, I shall focus with photographs. When images become inadequate, I shall be content with silence."  Ansel Adams

www.milla.de

www.blastradius.com

www.grafikonstruct.com.br

"You don't take a photograph, you make it."  Ansel Adams

www.sapient.com

"A true photograph need not be explained, nor can it be contained in words."

Ansel Adams

www.q-milk.de

"Photograph: a picture painted by the sun without instruction in art."

Ambrose Bierce

## Colour and transparency

Transparency is best thought of as a specific form of the contrast of saturation. Creating transparent layers involves shifting the colour values in those areas of the screen located "under" the transparency. The resulting palette always comes across as balanced and increases the potential for three-dimensional effects. Usually the proportion of white is increased so that the resulting tints appear raised and thus more in the foreground.

The surface's transparency reduces any contrasts present in the background enabling **text** to be rendered clearly, even against lively backgrounds. This enables different layers – perhaps representing levels of importance – to be blended in while keeping the central theme as a contextual indicator.

www.burntgraphix.com

**www.habitat.net**
Implementation of a video sequence as a transparent layer. The figure becomes visible only through its motion without obstructing the presented products.

**www.buero-linientreu.de**
By using effects of transparency, complex spatial arrangements can be represented in a way that remains coherent.

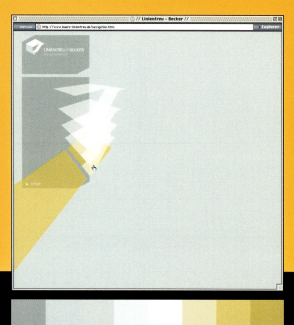

www.elastik.com.au

**www.nike.com/de**
The degree of transparency – and hence the prominence of the information – changes according to which area of the screen is currently active.

Transparent layers of colour are a good way of indexing different categories of information and provide the user with a useful means of reference. The resulting **colour mixtures** do not seem solid but are instead perceived as if they were a physical phenomenon i.e. actually transparent.

Overlaying multiple layers of transparency causes the **colour saturation** to increase and can be used to indicate visual density and frequency.

www.mid-tokyo.com

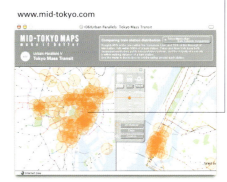

Additional semi-transparent layers of information remain visually distinct even where they overlap several times as the levels of saturation are combined at these points.

www.aamertaher.com

**www.mori.co.jp**
By using transparent layers of white to reduce the contrast of the background, blocks of text can be superimposed on patterns, textures or images. The opaque layer of white further increases the contrast between background and text and is hence an indicator for activation.

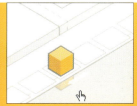

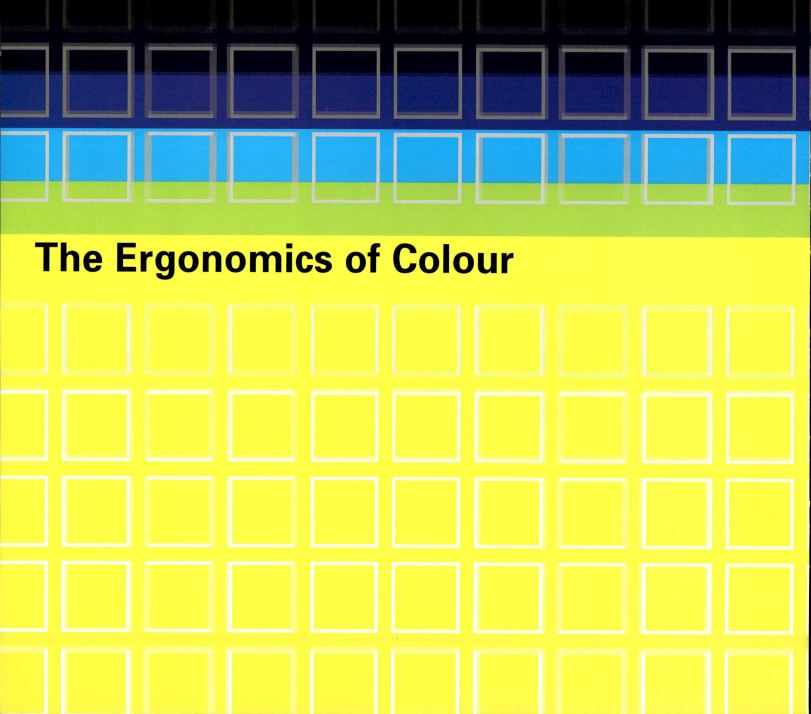

# The Ergonomics of Colour

1    2    3    4    5    6    7    8    9

Screen-based media are having more and more
impact on our daily lives. Increasingly information is
received in an on-screen format. Material presented
in this form places a greater strain on the eye than
would be the case with printed paper. When designing
for the screen, therefore, it makes sense to minimise
eye strain where possible so that viewing remains
comfortable.

**Text on the screen**

Low levels of resolution combined with low refresh rates make reading from a screen hard work. Practically everyone has experienced first hand how a thoroughly checked text can prove riddled with errors once printed out. Good choice of colour on the screen can contribute significantly to reducing strain on the eye. The "black and white" format is the heritage of the personal computer's first killer application: desktop publishing tries to simulate as closely as possible the printed page.

Screen-based forms of media emit light whereas paper simply reflects it. The **contrast in brightness** affected by combinations of colours is the most important consideration when trying to maximise readability. The 100% variation in brightness resulting from the use of black on white or white on black makes these formats unsuitable for extended periods of reading. In both instances the contours of the letters tend to bloom. A **discrepancy in brightness** of between 40 and 90% ensures easily readable text.

see also pages 88|89

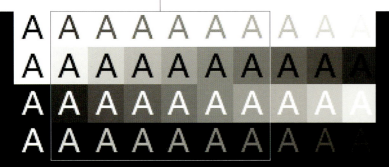

Since only the light parts of a screen are refreshed 50 to 100 times per second, white text on a black screen flickers far less than black type on a white screen.

A main layout theme of medium brightness allows the designer to work with lighter as well as darker typesetting.

The high intrinsic brightness of yellow makes it unworkable as a text colour on a white background. The same is true of white on yellow.

On the screen, equal levels of brightness cause text to disappear.

Rendering blue text on a dark grey or black background is impractical due to blue's intrinsically low levels of brightness.

www.hugeinc.com

www.carbonhouse.com

When rendering text over pictures or photos, transparent overlays are a good way of reducing the range of contrast present in the background and ensuring a certain uniformity of brightness contrast.

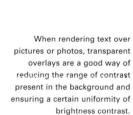

0%          25%          50%          75%          100%

The **simultaneous contrast** that results from using an achromatic text colour against a chromatic background can reduce a text's readability; a colour tone taken from the same **colour family** as that of the layout's background does not have this effect.

**Text on the screen**

Choice of font and type size are also factors affecting reading comfort. Typefaces with no variations in stroke thickness are easier to render on screen. As a rule, serif typefaces are best avoided for lengthy blocks of text. Used for decorative purposes, serif typefaces only work if rendered above a certain size. A general rule of thumb for type sizes: the smaller the type, the greater the brightness contrast – and hence the lower the chromatic contrast – should be set.

Using complementary colours at high saturation causes a very noticeable flickering effect. When reading at length, low-saturation colours are easier on the eye than high-saturation colours because the eye's receptors react more evenly to the light.

typography

typography

typography

typography

typography

typography

typography
48pt

typography
36pt

typography
24pt

typography
18pt

typography
14pt

typography
12pt

Anti-aliasing, a means of smoothing out edges by blurring them slightly, tends to make text come across as indistinct and ragged if used at a font size below 14pt. This makes reading difficult. On serif typefaces, this effect is evident even with larger type sizes.

Significant variations in stroke thickness of the sort often seen in serif typefaces makes reading on the screen hard work.

Sizes may well vary from typeface to typeface – Bodoni, for instance, comes up slightly smaller than Franklin Gothic despite the identical point size.

typography
48pt

typography
36pt

typography
24pt

typography
18pt

typography
14pt

typography
12pt

typography     typography

Anti-aliasing on complementary colours causes them to blur slightly at the edges.

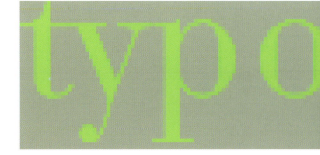

Anti-aliasing can cause the finer strokes in a font to break up.

# typography

# typography

## typography

### typography

### typography

### typography

typography
Trebuchet 11pt

typography
Andale Mono 10pt

typography
Verdana 9pt

TYPOGRAPHY
Silkscreen 9pt

TYPOGRAPHY
Mini 12pt

TYPOGRAPHY
Mini 12pt

# typography

## typography

### typography

### typography

#### typography

Typefaces such as Andale Mono or Silkscreen, which have been specially developed for use on the screen and as such are ideally suited to the idiosyncratic requirements of pixel-grid representation, are more robust. Pixel-based typefaces like Silkscreen are intended for use with a particular type size – 9pt in this case – and have been scaled down to offer upper case only.

The smaller the type size, the greater the brightness contrast should be. Anti-aliasing should also be avoided.

### typography

#### typography

##### typography

## Colour as an indicator for user interaction

Dynamic changes in colour tone, brightness, contrast and saturation can greatly enhance the navigational concept of a website. By reacting to the movements of the mouse cursor, alterations of this type can give the user feedback and aid orientation. From a design point of view, up to five different modes may be identified: where the **cursor** is positioned on a link, the interactive nature of the element is shown; as soon as the user **clicks**, a change confirms the system's "acknowledgement".

Once the **user has clicked**, the system signals that, say, an option on a menu has been selected; should the user leave a link without clicking, the screen component reverts to its original form; areas of a site **already visited** by the user may be highlighted in a distinctive way as well as **active** menu options. When designing, care should be taken to ensure that there is contextual congruity between the on-screen representation and what it signifies: activity can be shown by means of increased saturation, more colour, sharper focus or added contrast.

www.orisinal.org

www.navihedron.com

www.arthurmount.com

www.vonglitschka.com

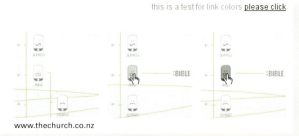

this is a test for link colors **please click**

www.10plus1.com

www.newatoday.com

www.thechurch.co.nz

www.crankmedia.com

www.massiveattack.co.uk

www.karimrashid.com

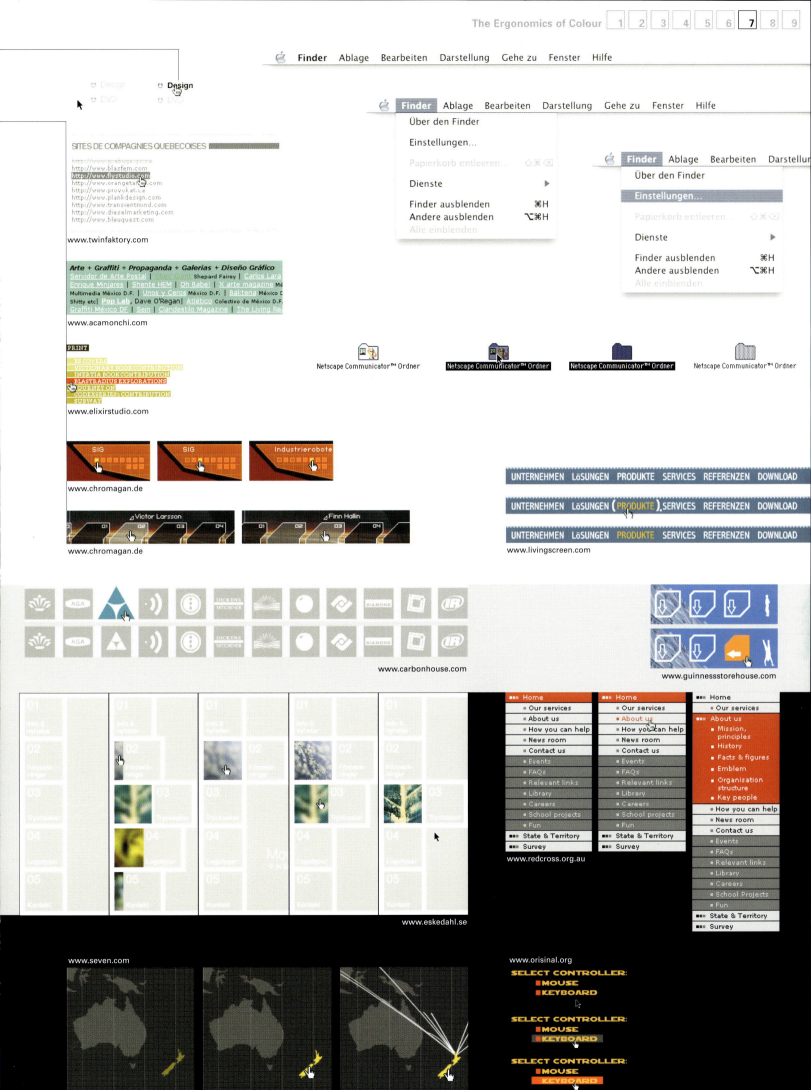

 Finder  Ablage  Bearbeiten  Darstellung  Gehe zu  Fenster  Hilfe

⏺ Design    ⏺ **Design**
⏺ DVD       ⏺ DVD

SITES DE COMPAGNIES QUEBECOISES

http://www.arabuga.qc.ca
http://www.blasfem.com
http://www.flystudio.com
http://www.orangetango.qc.ca
http://www.provokat.ca
http://www.plankdesign.com
http://www.transientmind.com
http://www.dieselmarketing.com
http://www.bleuquest.com

www.twinfaktory.com

**Arte + Graffiti + Propaganda + Galerías + Diseño Gráfico**
Servidor de Arte Postal |                    | Shepard Fairey | Carlos Lara
Enrique Minjares | Shente HEM | Oh Babe! | X arte magazine Mé
Multimedia México D.F. | Unos y Ceros México D.F. | Bakteria México D
Shitty etc| Pop Lab, Dave O'Regan| Atlético Colectivo de México D.F.
Graffiti México DF | Sein | Clandestilo Magazine | The Living Rea

www.acamonchi.com

PRINT
ZS COVERS
VICTIONARY BOOK CONTRIBUTION
INERTIA BOOK CONTRIBUTION
BLASTRADIUS EXPLORATIONS
JOURNEY ON
CODEXSERIES2 CONTRIBUTION
SUBWAY

www.elixirstudio.com

SIG    SIG    Industrierobote

www.chromagan.de

Victor Larsson    Finn Hallin
01 02    04        01    03    04

www.chromagan.de

 Finder  Ablage  Bearbeiten  Darstellung  Gehe zu  Fenster  Hilfe
Über den Finder
Einstellungen…
Papierkorb entleeren…          ⇧⌘⌫
Dienste                           ▶
Finder ausblenden              ⌘H
Andere ausblenden             ⌥⌘H
Alle einblenden

 Finder  Ablage  Bearbeiten  Darstellur
Über den Finder
Einstellungen…
Papierkorb entleeren…          ⇧⌘⌫
Dienste                           ▶
Finder ausblenden              ⌘H
Andere ausblenden             ⌥⌘H
Alle einblenden

Netscape Communicator™ Ordner    Netscape Communicator™ Ordner    Netscape Communicator™ Ordner    Netscape Communicator™ Ordner

UNTERNEHMEN  LöSUNGEN  PRODUKTE  SERVICES  REFERENZEN  DOWNLOAD

UNTERNEHMEN  LöSUNGEN ( PRODUKTE ) SERVICES  REFERENZEN  DOWNLOAD

UNTERNEHMEN  LöSUNGEN  PRODUKTE  SERVICES  REFERENZEN  DOWNLOAD

www.livingscreen.com

www.carbonhouse.com

www.guinnessstorehouse.com

www.eskedahl.se

▪▪▪ Home                ▪▪▪ Home                ▪▪▪ Home
▪ Our services          ▪ Our services          ▪ Our services
▪ About us              ▪ About us              ▪▪▪ About us
▪ How you can help      ▪ How you can help        ▪ Mission,
▪ News room             ▪ News room                 principles
▪ Contact us            ▪ Contact us              ▪ History
▪ Events                ▪ Events                  ▪ Facts & figures
▪ FAQs                  ▪ FAQs                    ▪ Emblem
▪ Relevant links        ▪ Relevant links          ▪ Organisation
▪ Library               ▪ Library                    structure
▪ Careers               ▪ Careers                 ▪ Key people
▪ School projects       ▪ School projects       ▪ How you can help
▪ Fun                   ▪ Fun                   ▪ News room
▪▪▪ State & Territory    ▪▪▪ State & Territory    ▪ Contact us
▪▪▪ Survey              ▪▪▪ Survey               ▪ Events
                                                ▪ FAQs
www.redcross.org.au                             ▪ Relevant links
                                                ▪ Library
                                                ▪ Careers
                                                ▪ School Projects
                                                ▪ Fun
                                                ▪▪▪ State & Territory
                                                ▪▪▪ Survey

www.seven.com

www.orisinal.org

SELECT CONTROLLER:
■ MOUSE
■ KEYBOARD

SELECT CONTROLLER:
■ MOUSE
■ KEYBOARD

SELECT CONTROLLER:
■ MOUSE
■ KEYBOARD

## Colour coding

Colour is ideal for adding structure to a layout – related subject matter can be colour coded and clearly marked off from other subject areas. On the Internet, where the complex array of links making up a website requires an intelligible structure, colour coding can be particularly helpful. If, however, more than six colours are used, difficulties begin to arise in labelling them and hence in clearly distinguishing one area from another.

It is essential to choose colours with similar levels of brightness and saturation otherwise each block of text combined with the layout will have to be handled separately to maintain readability. The same applies to any additional colours used to add emphasis, e.g. to highlight links.

www.relevare.com

www.rawfibre.co.uk

www.crowleywebb.com

www.volvocarsasia.com

www.brandeins.de

www.barneys.com

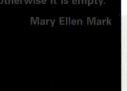

www.bauhaus.de

This type of indexing quickly creates very colourful effects that can dominate the overall theme of the layout. If, on the other hand, used too subtly, the **distinction** will no longer be apparent.

In order to ensure the clear distinction required for colour coding, certain quantities of each colour are needed. The more colours used, the closer their position to one another on the colour wheel and hence the greater the quantity needed to avoid uncertainty.

www.bauhaus-dessau.de

www.eightdotthree.net

## Colour coding information

The labelling of information is another important use of colour. The intuitive way our eyes react to colour contrasts can significantly accelerate the processing of information. The contrast of hue differentiates between types of information while the proportion of colour represents the quantity. Saturation is mostly used to show quantitative differences.

Of all combinations, yellow and black commands the attention of the viewer most effectively and is therefore commonly used as a warning in the real world and on the Internet.

www.tokyo-park.or.jp

www.airsensing.com

www.understandingusa.com

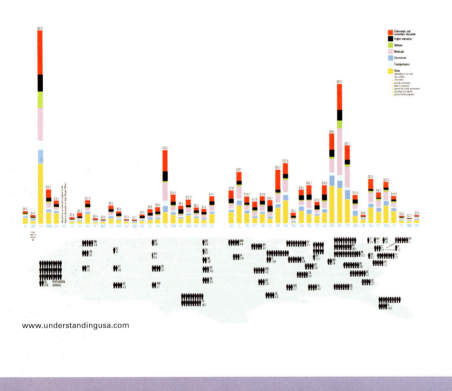

www.understandingusa.com

www.stauff.de

www.skyscraper.org

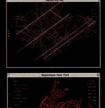

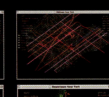

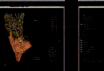

www.melair.com.au

**eHeimat**_interactive map
student project
S. Stage, C. Tiedge 2002

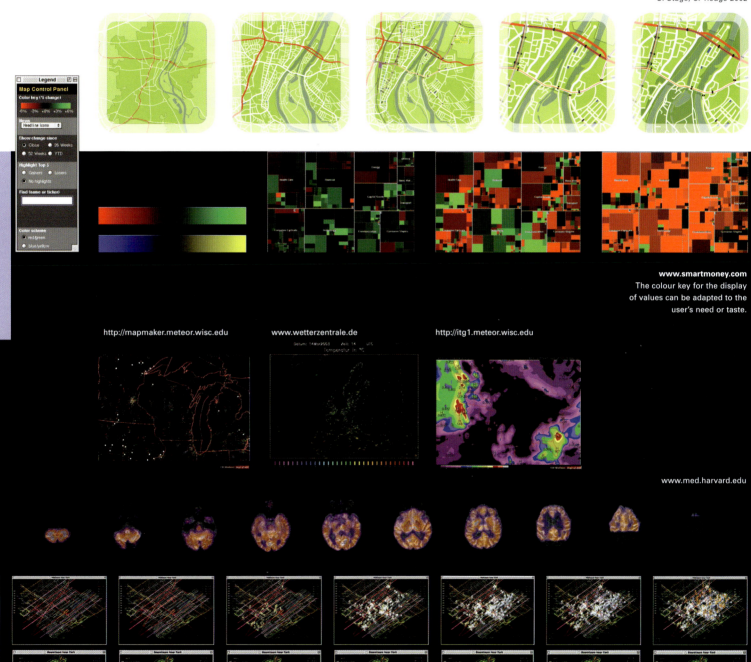

**www.smartmoney.com**
The colour key for the display
of values can be adapted to the
user's need or taste.

http://mapmaker.meteor.wisc.edu

www.wetterzentrale.de

http://itg1.meteor.wisc.edu

www.med.harvard.edu

## Architecture of a page

Colour is an important structural tool. Designing a Web page often entails dividing the available screen space up into function-specific zones. In most cases, a **navigational panel**, clearly separated from the **content**, will remain on hand.

Colour helps structure things logically and enables clear demarcation. Variations in levels of brightness may cause blocks of colour to either appear raised and in the foreground or to recede into the background resulting in a **layered effect**.

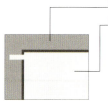

www.design-museum.de

**www.heymann-schnell.de**
The coloured squares, some quite dark, appear distinctly raised despite the light background. The effect is reinforced by a three-dimensional rotation of the blocks.

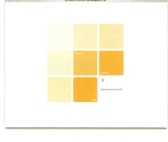

A classic layout with classic colour structuring. The menu in the form of a right angle along the left and top edges of the screen is characterised by high-saturation colour whereas the main content is rendered against a light background, in keeping with the text format seen in more traditional media.

www.whiskas.com

www.promarkt.de

www.nestle.com

www.opodo.de

www.golfweb.com

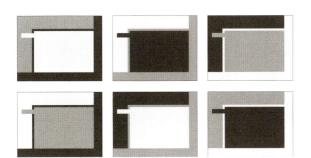

Depending on brightness levels, the foreground-background relationship undergoes a change: one moment the right-angle shaped menu appears raised in front of a backdrop, the next moment the light block appears to drift forwards from the dark background.

www.highrise.com

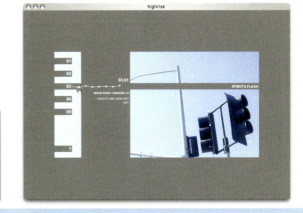

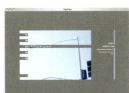

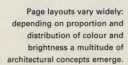

Page layouts vary widely: depending on proportion and distribution of colour and brightness a multitude of architectural concepts emerge.

www.carbonhouse.com

www.getpublic.ch

www.porsche.de

www.audi.com

www.madonna.com

www.morgenpost.berlin1.de

www.mori.co.jp

www.nikon.de

www.nike.com

117

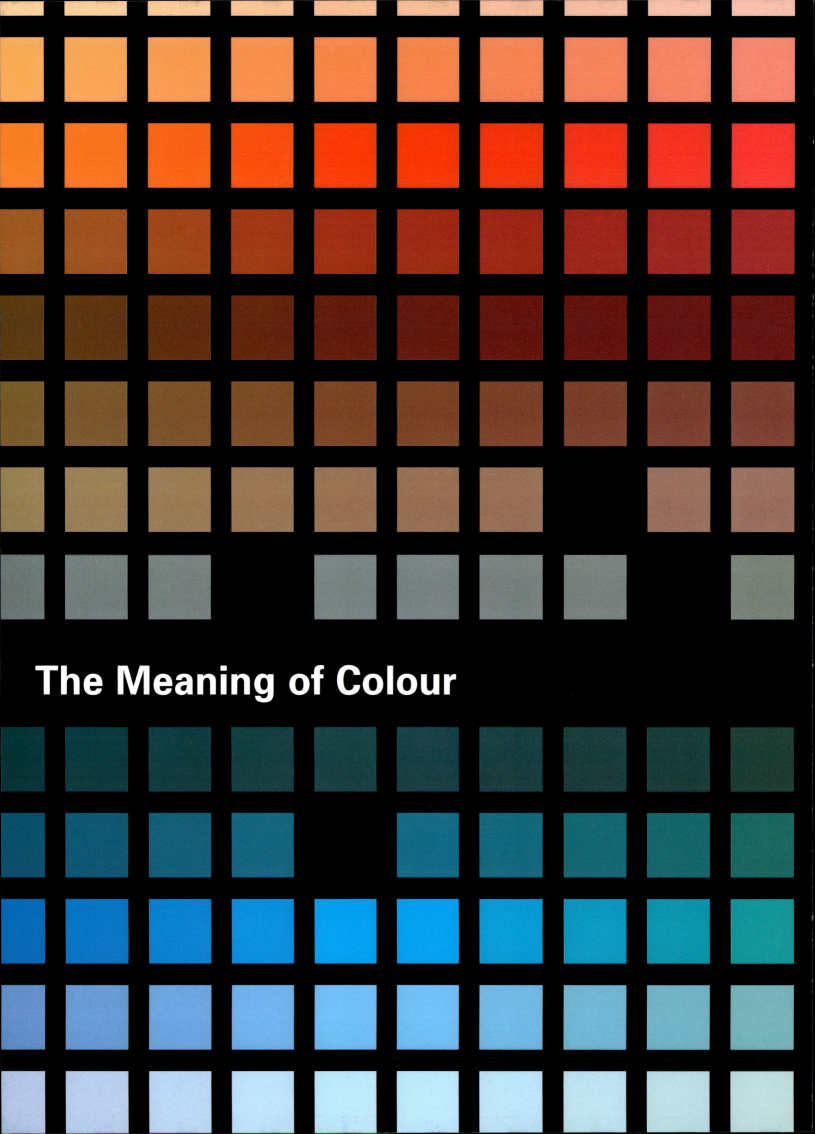

# The Meaning of Colour

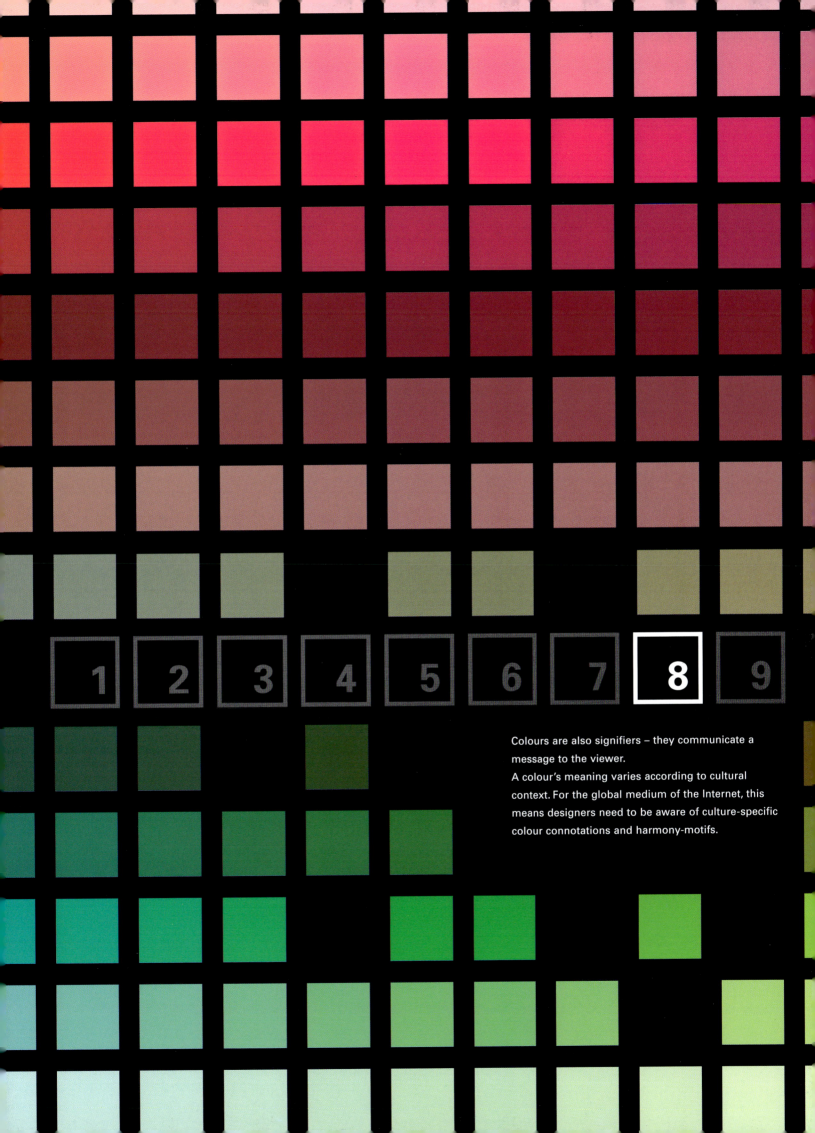

Colours are also signifiers – they communicate a
message to the viewer.
A colour's meaning varies according to cultural
context. For the global medium of the Internet, this
means designers need to be aware of culture-specific
colour connotations and harmony-motifs.

## Does tradition determine the colour palette?

Each colour has a history. Some colour tones were difficult to obtain or required extensive preparation, as a consequence they were very expensive. Other colours, taken from natural sources, were so common they tended to come across as boring to the eye. Several colours have been incorporated into language as idioms e.g. "green with envy", "to have the blues" etc. Colours, it would seem, are well suited to describing emotions and to the embellishment of language with vivid metaphor.

Many of these archaic associations have become lost, their relevance forgotten over the course of history so that they no longer influence the way a colour is seen. Other colour associations continue to affect perception at a collective level. Good choice of colour requires familiarity with this pool of meaning and the ability to draw on it creatively.

"Mere colour, unspoiled by meaning, and unallied with definite form, can speak to the soul in a thousand different ways."
Oscar Wilde

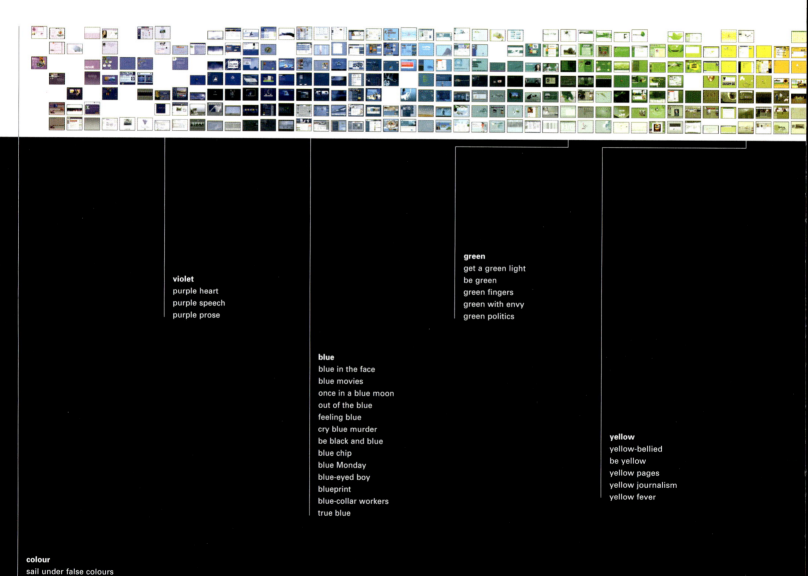

**violet**
purple heart
purple speech
purple prose

**green**
get a green light
be green
green fingers
green with envy
green politics

**blue**
blue in the face
blue movies
once in a blue moon
out of the blue
feeling blue
cry blue murder
be black and blue
blue chip
blue Monday
blue-eyed boy
blueprint
blue-collar workers
true blue

**yellow**
yellow-bellied
be yellow
yellow pages
yellow journalism
yellow fever

**colour**
sail under false colours
colour of money
show one's true colours
with flying colours
off colour

"That's my problem, chaplain: I'm yellow. PFC Bernstein – plumb, fat coward. Hey, can you get a Section 8 for being yellow?"

James Poe

Because a colour-meaning association tends to be formed in relation to a specific, usually high-saturation variant of a colour family, the associations invoked will become less distinct if indeterminate colours or more subtle gradations of tone value are used instead. Combinations of colours are likewise affected in this way. The contrast used is of similar importance in establishing a colour-meaning link and in determining the strength of an association.

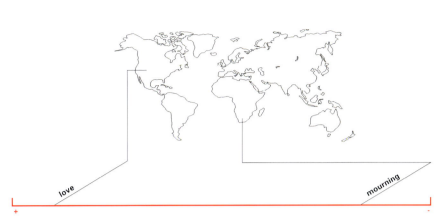

love                                    mourning
+                                              -

**Contemporary and traditional meanings** for a specific colour can range from good to bad. Therefore on the following pages those meanings and associations are distributed on a scale from **positive** to **negative**. Those associations that seem to manifest only in certain regions of the world are connected to those regions by indicating lines.

**pink**
pink power
rose-tinted glasses
pink-eye
tickled pink
pinkies
see pink elephants
rosy
be in the pink
the pink of elegance

**grey**
grey power
grey matter
grey area
grey economy

**white**
white lie
white elephants
white sale
white slavery
white Christmas
white flag
whitewash
white heat
white as a sheet
bleed white
white-collar workers
white water

**brown**
brown dwarf
brown out
brown nose
brown-bagging
browned off

**red**
red herring
paint the town red
red tape
red alert
in the red
red flag
red-letter day
see red
like a red rag to a bull
red cent
red hot
red neck
roll out the red carpet
red-faced
red-light district
catch someone red-handed
red-blooded
red dwarf

**black**
black market
black humour
black sheep
black and white
black-out
in the black
black look
black list
black spot
black book
black tie
black economy
blackball
blackmail
pot calling the kettle black
black ice
blackbox

## Violet

Violet is a colour stem inextricably bound up with traditional connotations. It comes across as having an air of extravagance and an almost complete disregard for respectability. This explains why high-saturation varieties are seldom used. A pale gradation of violet is typically thought of as appealing to a female target group of all ages.

The bulky dominance of the colour is what makes it interesting for the designer – it represents an unconventional choice and can be striking. Still, it is the accompanying colour contrasts that will really determine the overall effect of the colour.

www.biasfwd.com

www.mutts.co.jp

www.pineapplejazz.tk

www.avon.com

www.darcy.co.nz

www.unescape.com

www.sweetviolets.com

www.halfproject.com

www.arttattoo.ch

www.renvall.se

www.popmagazine.com

| | |
|---|---|
| Lavender | #E6E6FA |
| Indigo | #4B0082 |
| DarkViolet | #9400D3 |
| BlueViolet | #8A2BE2 |
| DarkOrchid | #9932CC |
| DarkSlateBlue | #483D8B |
| MediumOrchid | #BA55D3 |
| SlateBlue | #6A5ACD |
| MediumSlateBlue | #7B68EE |
| MediumPurple | #9370DB |
| Purple | #800080 |
| Orchid | #DA70D6 |
| Violet | #EE82EE |
| Plum | #DDA0DD |
| Thistle | #D8BFD8 |

www.serendipityphoto.com

www.amplified.nu

www.neuemedia.com

www.alchemyoffice.com

www.colour-balancing.de

www.riptideweb.com

www.atomic.net

www.firstcaribbeanbank.com

www.tele5.pl

www.national.com.au

www.muidlatif.cjb.net

www.fedex.com

fashionable · extravagant · magical · charming · feminine · creative · valuable · dignified · sensitive · **royal** · rank · loud · respectful · authority · ambiguous · old-fashioned · artificial · disreputable · indecisive · solitary · melancholic · decadent · static · **violence** · conscious · humility · **mourning** · vanity · arrogant · self-referential · extreme · deceptive · disloyal

www.bust.com

www.bluevioletmansion.com

"I think it pisses God off if you walk by the colour purple in a field somewhere and don't notice it."

Alice Walker

www.alien-nine.com

www.ala.org/teenhoopla

www.warnermusic.co.jp

www.drweb.at

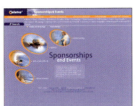
www.telstra.com

www.gdln.org

www.wildviolet.net

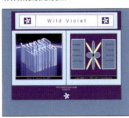
www.wildviolet.net

www.yr.com

www.bomee.com

www.hadw.com

www.whoismodi.com

www.sbu.ac.uk

www.barshow.co.uk

www.cittadellarte.it

www.content.com

www.exim.gov

www.ihearithurts.com

www.violetskin.com

www.violetskin.com

www.connected-earth.com

www.jnj.com

www.alcina-beautyshop.de

## Blue

Blue represents technology, precision and purposefulness and as such is the colour prefered by technology companies the world over. On the Internet, blue Is more abundant than any other colour.

This charismatic colour is echoed across a range of other spheres. While **physiological factors** make it particularly well suited to use as a background theme, it also charges a layout with a set of positive, medium-relevant associations.

see also pages 44|45

congenial   harmonious   friendly   positive   trust   reliable   infinite   longing   fantasy   dreams   relaxation   secure   quiet   clever   sensible   certain   prepared   independent   orderly   punctuality   truth   pride   courage   masculine   **strength**   sporty   concentration   *godly*   noble   performance   purpose   commitment   peace

"Blueness doth express trueness."
Ben Jonson

| | | |
|---|---|---|
| Navy | #000080 |
| DarkBlue | #00008B |
| MediumBlue | #0000CD |
| Blue | #0000FF |
| MidnightBlue | #191970 |
| DodgerBlue | #1E90FF |
| RoyalBlue | #4169E1 |
| SteelBlue | #4602D4 |
| SlateGrey | #708090 |
| LightSlateGrey | #778899 |
| CornFlowerBlue | #6495ED |
| DeepSkyBlue | #00BFFF |
| SkyBlue | #87CEEB |
| LightSkyBlue | #87DEFA |
| LightBlue | #ADD8E6 |
| LightSteelBlue | #B0C4DE |
| AliceBlue | #F0F8FF |
| GhostWhite | #F8F8FF |

www.axis-media.com

www.royalbankscot.co.uk

www.berlin-airport.de

www.anz.com

www.thethirdplace.com

www.turanalem.kz

www.bankofscotland.co.uk

www.un.org

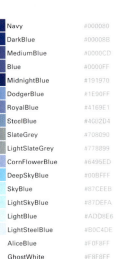

www.axis-media.com

www.sjd.co.nz

www.liquidcat.com

www.jewishmuseum.org

www.eltono.com

www.bluebyte.net

www.cobaltbc.com

www.hhconcept.de

www.bank.lv

www.braun.de

www.artistica.org

www.fovico.com

www.blauweiss-linz.at

www.newyorklife.com

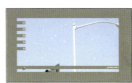
www.basicray.com

www.highrisedesign.com

www.bmg.com

www.loreal.de

www.designb.de

www.renatobello.com.br

www.allmaple.com

www.bio-mechanical.net

www.2advanced.com

authority   protection   water   heaven   cleanliness   depth   technology   constant   reserved   simple   calm   *gentle*   sympathetic   emotional   satisfied   naive   serious   distanced   static   constructive   hard   modest   *sad*   *mourning*   proletarian   inconspicuous   adaptation   *dishonesty*   *villainy*   slow   passive   unfeeling   cold

www.niveausa.com

www.stereotypography.com

www.hexal.de

www.bmo.com

www.ibm.com/de

www.coral.de

www.navy.org

www.clandrei.de

www.fleet.com

www.testpilotcollective.com

www.magic-kinder.com

www.zerokelvin.it

www.laeyeworks.com

www.mowax.com

www.syndicaat.org

www.nivea.com

www.klosterfrau.de

www.fascination.ch

www.banguat.gob.gt

www.wilkinson.de

www.webitosis.com

www.mysuper.watsonwyatt.com

www.droppod.com

www.cbs.com

www.popandpolitics.com

http://abc.go.com

www.cdicv.com

www.rodytrans.es

www.visa.com

www.redocal.com

www.bsx.com

www.lightguide.de

www.designmarathon.com

www.hondacars.com

www.ampira.com

# Cyan

The colour cyan is the most evocative tone in the blue colour stem. Cyan almost rivals blue in the popularity stakes and has similar qualities on the screen. It is visually unobtrusive and may therefore be used generously as part of a layout theme.

Pale gradations of cyan and combinations with white are a theme frequently chosen to represent technology companies as well as companies from the banking and insurance sectors.

www.lanka.net/centralbank

www.bam-b.com

www.superlooper.de

www.glassonion.com

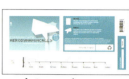
www.fantasmagoria.com

www.nowwashyourhands.com

www.rtl2.de

www.linkdup.com

www.kabeljau.ch

www.timrudder.com

www.milarepa.org

www.it-quadrat.de

www.idrica.com

www.wig-01.com

www.surfstation.lu

| | |
|---|---|
| MediumAquamarine | #66CDAA |
| Aquamarine | #7FFFD4 |
| PaleTurquoise | #AFEEEE |
| LightSeaGreen | #20B2AA |
| Turquoise | #40E0D0 |
| MediumTurquoise | #48D1CC |
| DarkSlateGrey | #2F4F4F |
| Teal | #008080 |
| DarkCyan | #008B8B |
| Cyan | #00FFFF |
| Aqua | #00FFFF |
| DarkTurquoise | #00CED1 |
| CadetBlue | #5F9EA0 |
| PaleTurquoise | #AFEEEE |
| PowderBlue | #B0E0E6 |
| LightCyan | #E0FFFF |
| Azure | #F0FFFF |

www.zoukclub.com

www.droppod.com

www.preloaded.com

http://sprite.cocacola.co.kr

www.urthgirl.com

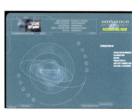
www.ambienceentertainment.com

www.loudblue.com

www.melair.com.au

www.panasonic.com

www.defrost.ca

www.lessrain.de

www.jeanpaulgaultier.com

www.bde.es

www.toei-anim.co.jp

http://purehydrogen.com

www.thehorusproject.com

www.gworka.com

breezy · light · liberating · open · refreshing · optimism · clear · alert · charming · composed · spontaneous · honest · congenial · playful · humorous · communication · hygienic · inspiration · self-knowledge · self-development · empathy · comradeship · graceful · cure · proactive · distanced · self-referential · empty

www.surfstation.lu

www.pantene.com/ko

www.pantene.com

www.chatswoodchase.com.au

www.bayer.de

www.wooribank.com

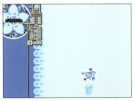

www.etherbrian.com

www.atlasmagazine.com

www.atlasmagazine.com

www.brainpop.com

www.leconfortmoderne.com

www.associatesinscience.com

www.guerriniisland.com

www.opencube.co.uk

www.wellatrendvision.com

www.fuelindustries.com

www.pbs.org/oceanrealm

www.thevoid.co.uk

www.fuse98.com

www.jvc.com

www.jeanpaulgaultier.com

www.hbo.com

www.pozzi-ginori.com

www.marcthiele.de

www.04.jp.org

www.tonicgroup.com

www.ny.frb.org

www.e-sh.ru

www.erivativesreview.com

www.doppiodesign.com

www.warnermusic.co.jp/supple

www.pixelleproject.com

www.breathnaigh.com

www.e-sh.ru

www.cirstra.com

## Green

The meaning attached to green varies greatly from culture to culture. While synonymous in arid desert-covered regions with ideas of paradise and revered in Islam as the colour of the prophet, green signifies femininity in China and wealth in America. Whether these associations are brought into play or not depends largely on levels of saturation and brightness.

Lime-green tones generally represent freshness, while darker, more forceful green tones are good for use in connection with a range of themes such as nature, ecology, chemistry and sport.

young　healthy　fresh　full　nature　life　spring　growth　fertility　power　hope　happiness　soothing　pleasing　go　neutral　strength　practical　theoretical

| | | |
|---|---|---|
| Chartreuse | #7FFF00 | |
| LawnGreen | #7CFC00 | |
| DarkGreen | #006400 | |
| Green | #008000 | |
| Lime | #00FF00 | |
| ForestGreen | #228822 | |
| OliveDrab | #6B8E23 | |
| DarkOliveGreen | #55682F | |
| GreenYellow | #ADFF2F | |
| YellowGreen | #9ACD32 | |
| LimeGreen | #32CD32 | |
| DarkSeaGreen | #8FBC8F | |
| LightGreen | #90EE90 | |
| PaleGreen | #98FB98 | |
| Honeydew | #F0FFF0 | |
| SpringGreen | #00FF7F | |
| MediumSpringGreen | #00FA9A | |
| SeaGreen | #2E8B57 | |
| MediumSeaGreen | #3CB371 | |

www.paradox.com

www.dtought.net

www.otago.ac.nz

www.innerval.com

www.gruene-fraktion.de

www.vasava.es

www.gruen-wirkt.de

www.garanti.com.tr

www.werder-online.de

www.die-farbe-gruen.de

www.muppetworld.com

www.fructis.de

www.kulturbolaget.se

www.hyro.com

www.joshmurray.com.au

www.threefiftyseven.com

www.buchananstreet.com

www.hi-res.net

www.smith-hawken.com

homepage.mac.com/samlind

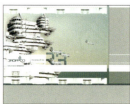
www.droppod.com

www.papeldigital.pt

www.mrdyms.com

www.cdpoly.com

www.planetofthedrums.com

www.caoz.com

www.novum.de

www.spakkamo.org

www.pacific.net.au

sure productive extravagant **material wealth, money** lush sensual wise just relaxation regeneration satisfied open perseverance protection concentration **catholic** holy immortal renewal helpful tolerant harmonious balance comfortable melancholic bitter harsh poisonous evil **unripe** aversion egoistic vile demon

www.mattjones.co.nz

www.discoverhomeloans.com.au

www.valkeus.com

www.barmer.de

www.goldtop.org

www.designbybuild.com

www.kids-station.com

www.superlooper.de

www.eurocreative.net

www.orisinal.org

www.surfacemedia.com.au

www.brightm.com.au

www.apak.com.au

www.barshow.co.uk

http://hanulyeoncha.cocacola.co.kr

www.apak.com.au/nomad

www.fugu.org

www.newworldodour.com

www.southparkmovie.com

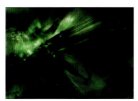
www.apak.com.au

www.gartentechnik.de

www.10plus1.com

www.surfstation.lu

www.milarepa.org

www.milla.de

www.crowleywebb.com

www.gruener-punkt.de

www.pop.org

www.lhw.com

www.orisinal.org

www.orisinal.org

www.greenpeace.org

www.neopod.net

www.stussystore.co.uk

## Yellow

Yellow is an optimistic, active and aggressive colour. Simply increasing or decreasing levels in the mix can cause the optimistic brightness of yellow-orange to shift into a sulphurous yellow-green. Its overtly eye-catching nature makes yellow instantly recognisable as a warning signal whatever the context. While few, there are cases where yellow is suitable as a main layout theme. It is best made use of sparingly on commercial websites to complement house colours where these form an integral part of the corporate identity.

"There are painters who transform the sun into a yellow spot, but there are others who, thanks to their art and intelligence, transform a yellow spot into the sun."

Pablo Picasso

Yellow is an unstable colour. Changing the weight of components or altering the brightness is enough to undermine the immediate impression of "yellow".

optimism · joyful · fun · gold · sunshine · amicable · heat · energy · active · fertile · cheerful · radiant · warm · liberating · stimulating · generous · **children** · conciliatory · fast

|  |  |
|---|---|
| Gold | #FFD700 |
| Olive | #808000 |
| DarkKhaki | #BDB76B |
| Yellow | #FFFF00 |
| DarkGoldenrod | #B8860B |
| Goldenrod | #DAA520 |
| Peru | #CD853F |
| BurlyWood | #DEB887 |
| Tan | #D2B48C |
| Khaki | #F0E68C |
| PaleGoldenrod | #EEE8AA |
| LemonChiffon | #FFFACD |
| LightGoldenrodYellow | #FAFAD2 |
| Beige | #F5F5DC |
| Cornsilk | #FFF8DC |
| LightYellow | #FFFFE0 |
| Oldlace | #FDF5E6 |
| Ivory | #FFFFF0 |

www.superlooper.de

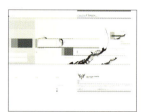
www.chapter3.net

www.nottsart.co.uk

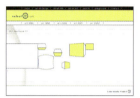
www.velvet.de

www.angeloplessas.com

www.gelbeseiten.de

www.rmxxx.com

www.quam.de

zeitungslab.fh-vorarlberg.ac.at

www.yellowstrom.de

www.duden.de

www.pixelsurgeon.com

www.futura.si

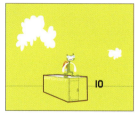
www.jotto.com

www.spat.com.au

www.mr-ka.de

www.jiong.com

www.greeningaustralia-wa.org

www.voi.com.au

www.halfproject.com

www.appliederivatives.com

www.ozemates.com.au

www.sfballet.org

www.halleck.com

www.tominwood.co.uk

www.viaduct.co.uk

www.handersonline.kit.net

www.studioeg.com

www.digit1.com

prosperity, earth, sun
happiness, fame, wisdom, harmony
grace
future
enlightenment
expensive, luxurious
progressive
intellect
lustre
protection
**caution**
**danger**
mellow
loud
extroverted
untroubled
careless
outrageous
sour
nervous
**cowardly**
**hesitant**
restless
unrealistic
**mourning**
egoism
crazy
obtrusive
uncongenial
problems
treachery
nausea
lies

www.weareshit.com

www.commerzbank.de

www.handsan.de

www.10plus1.com

www.deutschepost.de

www.dynax.com

www.superlooper.de

www.amoebalabs.com

www.teamuniform.net

www.rmxxx.com

http://carban.net

www.namco.co.uk

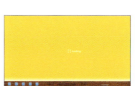
www.danpearlman.com

www.brightm.com.au

www.dosgringos.net

www.oportochicken.com.au

www.biffclothing.com

www.seven.co.nz

www.campquality.org

www.nowwashyourhands.com

www.ad.doubleclick.net

www.newwebpick.com

www.toei-anim.co.jp

http://members.surfeu.fi/mikko7

www.moccu.com

www.butter.cc

www.caffmag.com

www.amplified.nu

www.sustainable.net

www.72ppi.com

www.amnesty.org

www.ups.com

www.wordworth.com

www.artichokedesign.com.au

## Orange

Orange is a colour that seems able to evoke strong emotions. It somehow manages to create an impression of oscillating at intervals between pleasant optimism and budget trendiness. Classically used on the screen as a mode of emphasis for a website's navigation elements, the colour's high intrinsic brightness coupled with its warm positioning on the colour wheel help pick it out against a range of backgrounds and bring it to the foreground of the screen.

## Brown

The brown scale spans a range of colours from the deep yellow-green of olive through to the reddish-orange rust colours. As a screen background, layouts based on light gradations of beige are popular. These colours dampen brightness, reduce text-background contrast and are composed of roughly equal proportions of light emission from each of the three colour dots comprising a pixel. These natural-looking colours are common in connection with a variety of topics including hotels, lifestyle and culture.

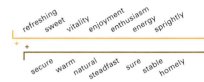

refreshing  sweet  vitality  enjoyment  enthusiasm  energy  sprightly

+

secure  warm  natural  steadfast  sure  stable  homely

*"How beautiful the leaves grow old. How full of light and colour are their last days."*
John Burroughs

www.trixi2.com

http://homepages.ihug.com.au

www.sportfreunde-stiller.de

www.artgrowden.com

www.trixi2.com

www.freshthrills.com

www.discovertoys.com

www.radioeins.de

www.cooty.net

| | |
|---|---|
| OrangeRed | #FF4500 |
| DarkOrange | #FF8C00 |
| Orange | #FFA500 |
| Chocolate | #D2691E |
| SaddleBrown | #8B4513 |
| Sienna | #A0522D |
| SandyBrown | #F4A460 |
| DarkSalmon | #E9967A |
| LightSalmon | #FFA07A |
| NavajoWhite | #FFDEAD |
| Wheat | #F5DEB3 |
| Moccasin | #FFE4B5 |
| PeachPuff | #FFDAB9 |
| Bisque | #FFE4C4 |
| BlancheAlmond | #FFEBCD |
| PapayaWhip | #FFEFD5 |
| AntiqueWhite | #FAEBD7 |
| Linen | #FAF0E6 |
| Seashell | #FFF5EE |
| FloralWhite | #FFFAF0 |

www.mokarabia.com

www.innerblitz.com

www.enzymedesign.com.au

www.derush.net

www.voi.com.au

http://skyscraper.paregos.com

www.simian.nu

www.mokarabia.com

www.planetalboran.com

www.ewtn.com

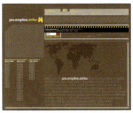
www.preemptivestrike.nu

www.fluffco.com

www.vatican.va

www.lunapod.com

www.philterdesign.com

www.kantemusik.de

http://opaldust.com

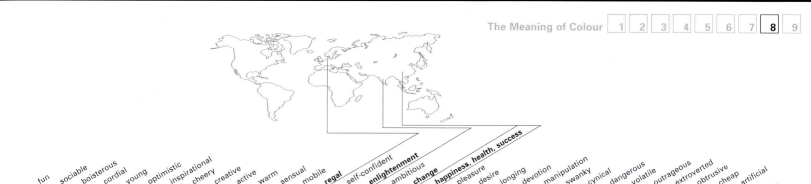

fun   sociable   boisterous   cordial   young   optimistic   inspirational   cheery   creative   active   warm   sensual   mobile   **regal**   self-confident   **enlightenment**   ambitious   **change**   **happiness, health, success**   pleasure   desire   longing   devotion   manipulation   swanky   cynical   dangerous   volatile   outrageous   extroverted   obtrusive   cheap   artificial

engaged   **cosy**   traditional   aromatic   conformist   mediocre   reserved   shy   unfriendly   conservative   **German**   square   conventional   unerotic   inconspicuous   subordinate   poor   dull   indifferent   inactive   close   clumsy   stupid   lazy   passive   dirty   spoilt   old   dry   bitter   inedible   evil   guilt   death

*"Fall is my favorite season in Los Angeles,*
*watching the birds change colour and fall from the trees."*

David Letterman

www.refugeedesign.org

www.balance-muenchen.de

www.bankofgeorgia.com.ge

www.warnermusic.co.jp/sinba

www.10plus1.com

www.disfunktional.com

www.nedstatbasic.net

www.bumper.com

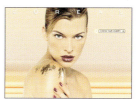

www.lorealparis.com

www.crowley-webb.com

www.whoismodi.com

www.propagandaonline.com

www.egomedia.com

www.mycity.com.br

www.brightm.com.au

www.mojotown.com

www.plastic-surgery-chicago.com

www.egomedia.com

www.massive.com

www.zoomfilmtv.com.au

www.nequo.net

www.purefusion.com

www.kvad.com

www.halfproject.com

www.ewitewit.com

www.dstrukt.net

www.hyro.com

www.surfstation.lu

www.goldenshower.gs

www.gutterandstars.com

# Red

Red is an active, dynamic colour. The ideas connected with it span happiness, love and danger. Whether used as an eye-catcher for jostling special offers in the retail or service sectors or as a warning signal, high-saturation variants of this colour are a surefire way to grab the attention.

Using companies' house colours on the net to pick out navigation elements or underpin the layout structure has become fairly common practice. Completely red backgrounds are predominantly used in the entertainment sector, say, by television broadcasting companies, and evoke the red curtain of the theatre.

love  passion  lust  erotic  desire  excitement  affection  happiness  fertility  enthusiasm  **wedding**  *joy*  vivacious  seduction  energy  heat, warmth  power  motivation  conquest

www.asifkhan.co.uk

www.motivdesign.com

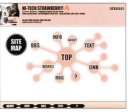
www.cyberoz.net

www.arteria.com

www.surfstation.lu

www.lobo.cx

www.weareshit.com/heroin

www.raumrot.de

www.nellyfurtado.com

www.feuerwehr.de

www.logictivity.com

www.jiong.com

www.cocacola.co.jp

www.metadesign.de

www.rosso-bianco.de

| | |
|---|---|
| Maroon | #800000 |
| DarkRed | #8B0000 |
| Red | #FF0000 |
| FireBrick | #B22222 |
| Brown | #A52A2A |
| Tomato | #FF6347 |
| Coral | #FF7F50 |
| IndianRed | #CD5C5C |
| Salmon | #FA8072 |
| LightCoral | #F08080 |
| RosyBrown | #BC8F8F |
| MistyRose | #FFE4E1 |
| Snow | #FFFAFA |

www.oregon.org

www.spd.de

www.ambit3.com

www.prosieben.de

www.mecompany.com

www.nbc.com

www.premiere.de

www.vox.de

www.karborn.com

www.volumeone.com

www.clubrisk.nl

http://fingertips.newdamage.com

www.missionimpossible.com

www.whoismodi.com

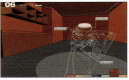
www.effraction.free.fr

www.diesel.com

www.halfproject.com

www.brick-by-brick.com

"If you can't make it good make it big.
If you can't make it big make it red."

Paul Rand

active  strong  vitality  dynamic  attractive  **valuable, beautiful**  **communism**  feminine  glowing  extrerne  self-confident  belligerent  dominant  loud  dubious  **mourning**  disreputable  **stop**  clashing  sharp  vicious  aggressive  **evil**  hate  fury  blood  sin  power  danger  war  hell  devilish  forbidden  hectic

www.creolab.com

www.moluv.com

www.santander.pt

www.todcorporation.com

www.zellteilung.de

www.raumrot.de

www.ghetto.pl

www.droppod.com

www.hektik.com.au

www.extra.jp.org

www.columbia.jp

www.52mm.com

www.milknosugar.com

www.hektik.com.au

www.francoischalet.ch

www.redsquare.com

www.world-crisis.de

www.emoem.com

www.mokarabia.com

www.headfirstsolutions.com

http://fingertips.newdamage.com

www.typographic.com

www.omniaband.com

www.visive.com

www.redcanyon.com

www.metalshop.com

www.typographic.com

www.maranellorosso.com

www.maranellorosso.com

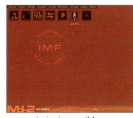
www.missionimpossible.com

www.the-rev.com

www.seven.com

www.desirebrandmanagement.com

www.laurentz-design.com

www.hayfieldrobinson.com

135

## Magenta

The colour magenta carries connotations similar to those of violet. The tint variants stand for naivety and romanticism. High-saturation variants of magenta represent a cooler alternative to red and are therefore often used as a mode of emphasis by technology companies.

tender    innocent    soft    easy    feminine    gentle    harmonious    charming    hopeful

www.davidbowie.com

www.linkclub.or.jp

www.futurefarmers.com

www.10plus1.com

www.eltono.com

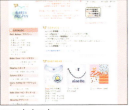
www.babys-b.com

www.ume.sakura.ne.jp

www.ladymisskier.info

www.gelbeseiten.de/telefon

www.alien-nine.com

www.giorgio-armani.com

www.riptideweb.com

www.ladymisskier.info

www.gasketmedia.com

www.rochfort.com

www.lab01.com

www.az2.co.uk

www.az2.co.uk

www.pinkdot.com

| | |
|---|---|
| DarkMagenta | #8B008B |
| Magenta | #FF00FF |
| Fuchsia | #FF00FF |
| DeepPink | #FF1493 |
| Crimson | #DC143C |
| MediumVioletRed | #C71585 |
| HotPink | #FF69B4 |
| PaleVioletRed | #DB7093 |
| LightPink | #FFB6C1 |
| Pink | #FFC0CB |
| Lavenderblush | #FFF0F5 |

www.physikdesign.com

www.hannover.de

www.hyro.com

www.twu.co.nz

www.screenloft.com

www.physikdesign.com

www.joshandcandice.com

www.zitrones.com

"Pink is the Navy Blue of India."
Diana Vreeland

grateful  healthy  delightful  pleasant  mild  amiable  homosexual  friendly  happy  young  naive  modest  idealism  meditation  perfection  romantic  dreams  fancy  sentimental  longing  zest  erotic  sexuality  compromise  renunciation  adaptation  material  uncertain  artificial  inappropriate  dominant  arrogant  vain

www.10plus1.com

www.superlooper.de

www.surfstation.lu

www.telekom.de

www.futurefarmers.com

www.eurocreative.net

www.zootydesign.com

www.fantazmagloria.com

www.ap-art.co.uk

www.bebe.de

www.az2.co.uk

www.weareshit.com

www.studioanybody.com

www.velvet.de

www.linglingshop.com

www.idnworld.com

www.unescape.com

www.az2.co.uk

www.werde-informatikerin.de

www.linevision.de

www.boo-jazz.de

www.devicefonts.co.uk

www.younggunsdesign.com

www.loreal.com

http://pondok.iinet.net

www.surfstation.lu

www.ala.ch

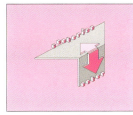
www.superlooper.de

www.btm.co.jp

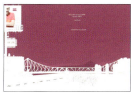
www.mapmagazine.com.au

www.pinknoises.com

www.unescape.com

www.bbc.co.uk

## White

The colour white is very commonly used on the screen as a main layout theme. White represents a neutral page colour suggestive in appearance of printed-media. White is also colourless and forms a neutral relationship with the other colours in a layout. On the Internet, white stands for purposefulness, objectivity and functionality. The trouble with using white as a layout background lies in the fact that it is the reversal of the technical principles that screens are based upon and is therefore **ergonomically inappropriate** for the media.

see also pages 106|107

## Grey

The colour grey, used at low brightness levels, gives an appearance of neutrality. Depending on how levels of brightness are set and the interplay of contrasts, the impression can either be one of elegant silver-grey functionality or of unaffected, prosaic banality.

light   honest   eternal   absolute   wise   purposeful   unequivocal   true   reincarnation   **purity**   **immortality**   quiet   modern   elegant   festive   ideal   innocent   wedding   trustworthy   meek   accurate

"White...is not a mere absence of colour; it is a shining and affirmative thing, as fierce as red, as definite as black...God paints in many colours; but He never paints so gorgeously, I had almost said so gaudily, as when He paints in white."

G. K. Chesterton

| Silver | #C0C0C0 |
| LightGrey | #D3D3D3 |
| Gainsboro | #DCDCDC |
| WhiteSmoke | #F5F5F5 |
| White | #FFFFFF |

www.frontend-multimedia.com

www.pentagram.com

www.thechurch.co.nz

www.artrafal.com

www.guggenheim-bilbao.es

www.objectsofdesire.de

www.fatoe.com

www.fourm.com

www.postpanic.nl

www.bornmagazine.org

www.industryfilms.com

www.opaldust.com

www.raster.art.pl

www.velvet.de

http://ps3.praystation.com

www.superlooper.de

www.zitrones.com

www.mindmeldcreative.com

www.wemfg.com

sure  simple  good  beginning  elementary  modest  pious  clever  new  functional  **monarchy**  belief  beginning  clean  winter  order  sterile  space  frigid  cold  solitary  **sorrow**  **mourning**  impersonal  illusary  unready

functional  purposeful  clever  punctual  civilised  independent  considerate  enigmatic  festive  modern  elegant  expensive  splendid  indefinite  modest  clear  neutral  plain  **serious**  solitary  unconsoled  calm  **monotone**  cloudy  introverted

"It is only after years of preparation that the young artist should touch colour – not colour used descriptively, that is, but as a means of personal expression."

Henri Matisse

www.zxero.cjb.net

www.aamertaher.com

www.orangebleu.net

www.lostpixel.com

www.mundidesign.com

www.tominwood.co.uk

www.armeirre.de

www.onyro.com

www.01-la-com

www.crowleywebb.com

www.owenlogic.com

www.warnermusic.co.jp/babyboo

www.soulbath.com

http://xururu.org

www.thethirdplace.com

www.insomne.iespana.es

www.soulbath.com

www.3ermundo.com

www.bionic-systems.com

www.newstoday.com

www.info-it.pl

www.designer-poster.com

http://homepage.mac.com/bish73

www.paulkellydesign.com

www.banksy.co.uk

## Black

The colour black is the natural condition of the screen. A black theme used as background tends to work well and as such represents the obvious choice for the medium. The connotations of this colour are, however, such that considerations of functionality ought to be secondary. When using black, care needs to be taken to ensure the various colour components of a layout combine well and are correctly proportioned otherwise negative associations result e.g. emptiness, mourning and misfortune.

Used well, black can help reinforce the effect of other colours, increase the brilliance of a layout and communicate elegance and modernity.

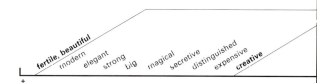

+ fertile, beautiful / modern / elegant / strong / big / magical / secretive / distinguished / expensive / creative

unfeeling / uncertain / prosaic / square / conventional / conformist / mediocre / banal / dull / sober / unfriendly / cold / old-fashioned / poor / cheap / unnatural / secret / dry / hard / bad / cool / winter / insincere / miserly / humility / misery / emptiness

"Concrete is, essentially, the colour of bad weather."

William Hamilton

| | |
|---|---|
| Black | #000000 |
| DimGrey | #696969 |
| Grey | #808080 |
| DarkGrey | #A9A9A9 |

www.rinzen.com

www.absolute-media.net

www.artszone.net

www.michaelnajjar.com

www.suffocate.org

www.q-milk.de

www.suprememundane.com

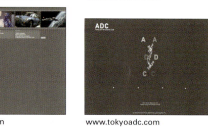
www.kraftwerk.com

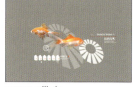
www.the-control-group.com

www.wireframe.co.za

www.edenfx.com

www.tokyoadc.com

www.artdirectorsanonymous.com

www.ego7.com

www.eltono.com

www.designgraphik.com

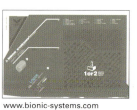
www.bionic-systems.com

www.shellmoonsite.com

www.panism.com

www.seven.co.nz

functional  purposeful  powerful  solitary  rebellious  conservative  introverted  forbidden  unequivocal  decisive  cold  heavy  narrow  pessimism  angular  arrogant  hopelessness  threatening  dark  empty  impenetrable  closed  brutal  hard  malicious  egoistic  unfaithful  insincere  misfortune  bad luck  death  mourning  end

"An American can have a Ford in any colour so long as it's black."

Henry Ford

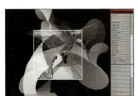
www.natzke.com

www.erikrefner.dk

http://geocities.com/jumble_667

http://opaldust.com

www.gucci.com

http://angeloplessas.com

www.akayism.org

www.nanogod.org

www.tominwood.co.uk

www.willing-to-try.com

www.giorgio-armani.com

www.rojola.nl

www.zone4.com.au

www.armstrong-consultants.com

www.grundrauschen.de

www.swift3d.com

www.stoav.be

www.obeygiant.com

www.atelierkontrast.de

www.droppod.com

www.designisdead.be

www.65media.com

www.space-invaders.com

www.imaginaryforces.com

www.kraftwerk.com

**One company, many colours**

A worldwide operating corporation usually has a unified corporate design concept. This includes the choice and use of colours. Often enough though the local implementation has to take the cultural specifics into account. Even a seemingly unquestionable colour like blue or grey, the corporate colours in this case, cannot be implemented regardless of the local cultural background.

The corporation might be positioned differently in different markets or countries. It might not be prudent to constantly stress the technical aspect, embodied by the cool grey/ silver/ blue palette. In the **USA** the corporation stresses its entertainment factor with a vivid orange.

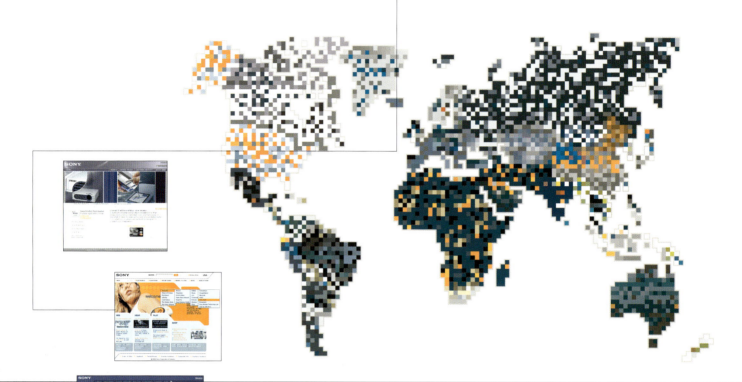

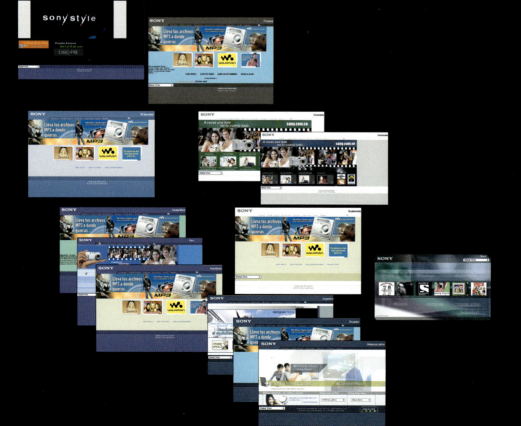

Also the blue itself varies regionally by saturation,
brightness and hue; although the sites facilitate
common data and pictures, and many sites are just
available in English.

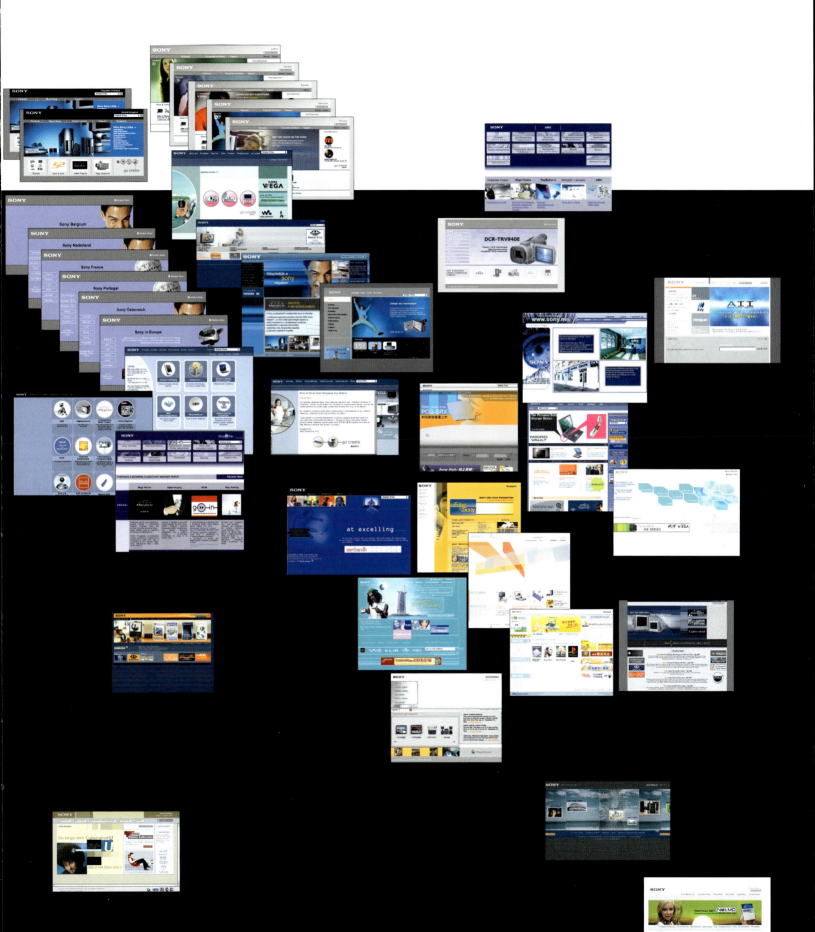

## Industry colours: banking

The traditional meaning of colours is diminishing in significance yet there are tendencies for certain sectors to use certain colours. While multimedia agencies seek to get attention through unconventional use of colour, other industry sectors are less willing to experiment, preferring to communicate values such as reliability and seriousness. Take, for example, the banking sector, which sticks in its majority to the preferred blue and white scheme.

Using other colours for this sector will immediately strike one as unusual. Indeed, even a rejigging of **the colour components** in favour of the blue tone from 1/3 to 2/3 is seldom to be found. Exceptions are only found in **local economies** where different banks stick to distinct colour families in an attempt to set themselves apart from their competitors.

www.snb.ch

www.bct.gov.tn

www.mercantil.com.do

www.icbc.com.tw

www.bankrakyat.com.my

www.bahisl.com.bh

www.degroof.be

www.deutsche-bank.de    www.dresdner-bank.de    www.commerzbank.de    www.sparkasse.de

www.btm.co.jp

www.friba.nl    www.nbs.co.za    www.mkb.hu    www.kvb.co.in

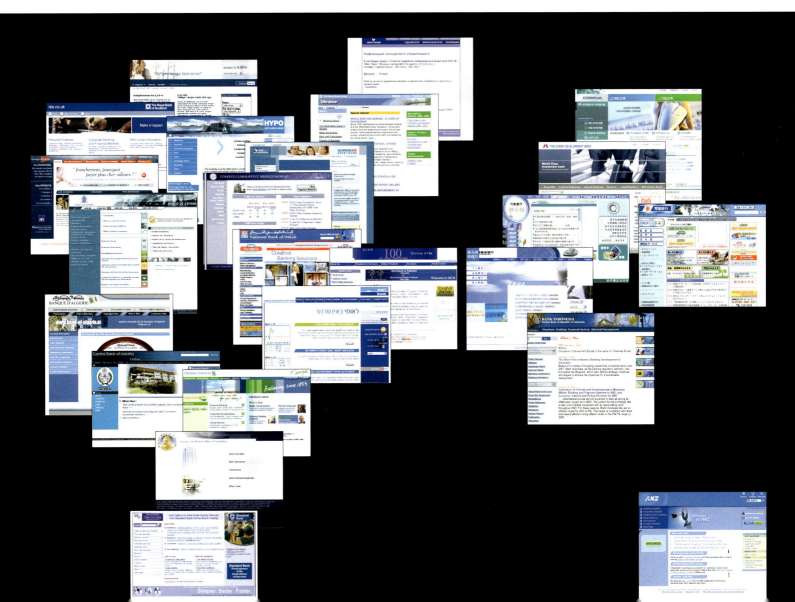

# Dynamic colour

The way we see colour is subjective and constantly changing.

In digital media, colour doesn't necessarily have to be fixed – factors such as time and user interaction may directly influence the colour composition of a page. This chapter demonstrates the ways these factors can be used to manipulate colour.

## Dynamic colour

The effects of colour are hugely dependent on time of day and lighting conditions. We often fail to notice the variations at a conscious level, our **visual apparatus** works to compensate for a lot, yet this mutability is characteristic of our daily surroundings.
Digital media are able to simulate this phenomenon by using subtle variations in colour to create a range of different lighting and atmospheric effects that might not get noticed except in passing yet contribute to the energy of the presentation.

see also pages 22|23

see also pages 100|101

**www.mori.co.jp**
This property agent's website enhances presentations of building proposals by using an ongoing shift in lighting mode and colour temperature to simulate the time of day.

**www.thechemicalbrothers.com**
The background colours fluctuate very subtly, running through the colours of the oxidation process.

www.madxs.com

www.spill.net

"The Mediterranean has the colour of mackerel, changeable I mean. You don't always know if it is green or violet, you can't even say it's blue, because the next moment the changing reflection has taken on a tint of rose or grey."

Vincent van Gogh

**iTunes**
The digital music player creates abstract animations based on music played through it.

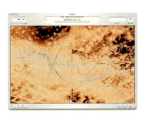   

www.liminalstudio.com

**www.designunion.net**
Interactive animations making use of white filters to create effects of constantly changing backlighting.

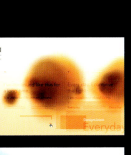

## Interactive colour

One idea to which the medium lends itself particularly well is that of allowing users to choose the colour scheme themselves. In this way individual preferences and physical limitations such as **colour blindness** can be catered for. This feature has so far only been incorporated into more experimental sites though there are one or two exceptions.

The range of choice offered should be limited to ensure suitable margins of contrast between context and information.

see also pages 28|29

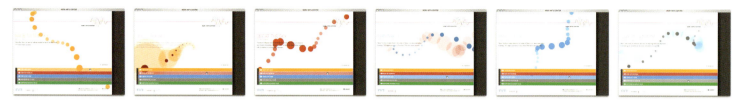

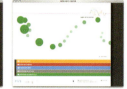

**www.moriartscenter.org**
When navigating the site, the colour-coded menu also determines the colour of the background animation.

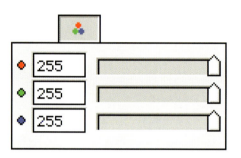

Colour pickers in websites are usually based on an RGB system. Combinations based on the additive colour system are much more difficult for the eye to predict than ones based on the subtractive system.

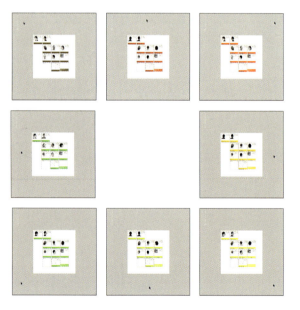

**www.virtualsuspects.com**
Based on a principle like that of the HSB system, where colours are assigned a numerical value corresponding to their angle on the colour wheel, the colour theme on this website changes according to the cursor's position on the page.

www.typospace.com

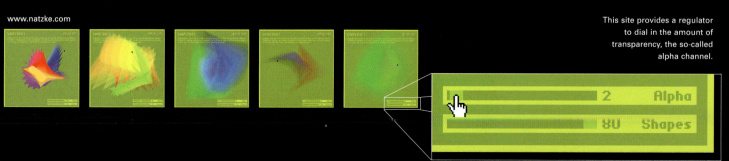

www.natzke.com

This site provides a regulator to dial in the amount of transparency, the so-called alpha channel.

An RGB regulator can be built in fairly easily
without an in-depth knowledge of programming.
However, because the eye does not have an intuitive
sense for combining additive colours, it is difficult
to get the right mix and the user will have to
experiment a while.

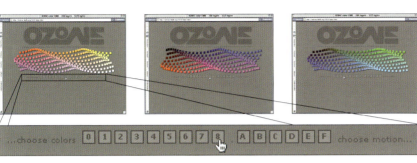

**http://entries.the5k.org**
Here, the user can choose from
nine pre-set colour combinations.

**www.digitlondon.com**
Choice of background theme
causes the colours to change,
influencing the overall effect.

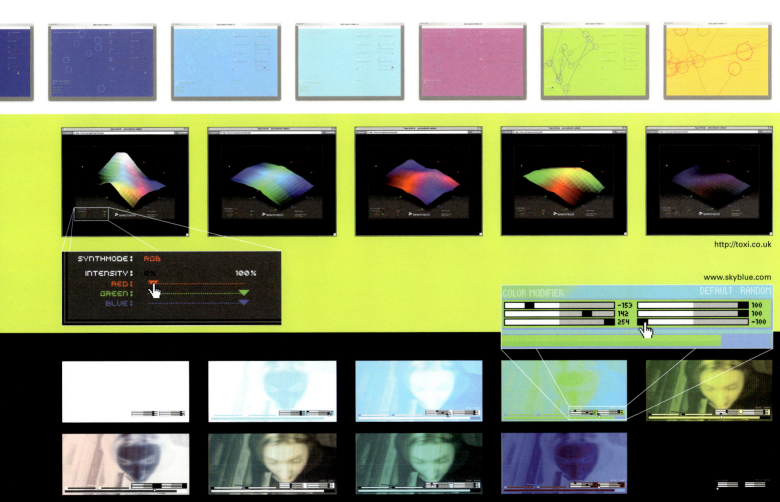

http://toxi.co.uk

www.skyblue.com

## Colour as a topic on the Internet

Colour is a fascinating subject and so it's hardly surprising that there are several sites devoted to it on the Internet. Using colour on the screen doesn't cost anything, which means the medium lends itself especially well to experimentation with colour: colour quantities and contrasts can easily be sampled and checked, say, for readability.

Some sites offer decision-making guides, which suggest and simulate colour **combinations**. Additionally, there are **stylised tools** available on the net, which can be used as support software when choosing colours.

www.colorcube.com/play

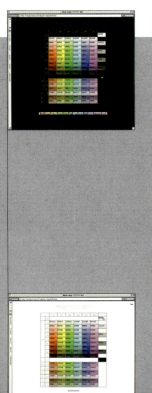
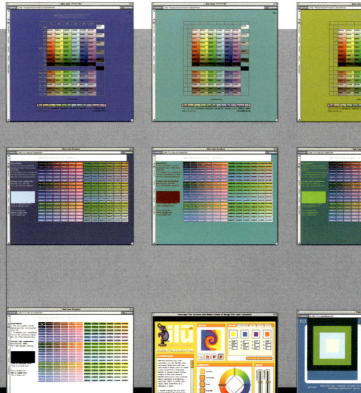

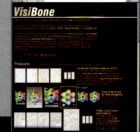

http://noz.day-break.net/webcolor    www.ideo.com/visualizer    www.sessions.edu    www.paletteman.com    www.visibone.com

http://acept.la.asu.edu/PiN/rdg/color
http://grammatik.free.fr/Farben
http://hotwired.lycos.com/webmonkey
http://noz.day-break.net/webcolor
http://pixxelpower.de/pages/grafik
http://telelab.mi.fh-offenburg.de/Vorlesung/Wahrnehmungspsychologie
world.std.com
www.8bit-museum.de
www.adobe.com/support/techguides/color
www.augeninfo.de
www.baunetz.de/sixcms/sixcms_4/sixcms/list.php?page_id=2135
www.beta45.de
www.cgsd.com/papers/gamma
www.cis.rit.edu/mcsl/faq
www.colorcombo.com
www.colorcube.com
www.colormall.com
www.colormatch.dk
www.colormatters.com
www.colorschemer.com/online
www.colorsystem.com
www.copyshop-tips.de
www.dotparagon.com
www.educat.hu-berlin.de/kurse/multimedia/grafik
www.etymologie.info/et/etfarben
www.farbe.com
www.farbenlehre.com
www.farbmetrik-gall.de
www.forum-entwerfen.de/forum/2/34
www.goethe.li
www.hhmi.org
www.ideo.com/visualizer
www.kopcom.com
www.kunstwissen.com
www.library.thinkquest.org
www.metacolor.de
www.mundidesign.com
www.munsell.com
www.paletteman.com
www.palettepicker.com/colorpicker
www.phaenomen-farbe.com
www.sessions.edu/ilus/#1
www.stud.uni-wuppertal.de/~ya0023/phys_psy/auge
www.thetech.org
www.thinkquest.org
www.toxi.co.uk
www.uni-regensburg.de/EDV/Misc/CompGrafik/Script_5
www.visibone.com
www.web-media.at/221858

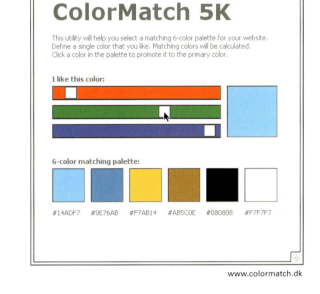

www.colormatch.dk

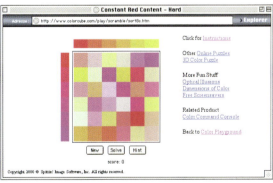

www.colorcube.com/play

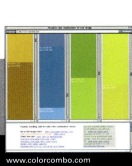

www.colorschemer.com/online    www.colorcombo.com    www.beta45.de    www.mundidesign.com    www.palettepicker.com

Werner Gilde. **Licht und Schatten**. Physik-Verlag, 1983

I.D. Atramonow. **Optische Täuschungen**.
Verlag Harri Deutsch, 1998

Richard L. Gregory. **Auge und Gehirn/Psychologie des Sehens**. Rowohlt, 2001

Thomas Ditzinger. **Illusionen des Sehens**.
Südwest Verlag, 1997

Ernst Peter Fischer. **Die Wege der Farben**.
Regenbogen Verlag Klaus Stromer, 1994

Narciso Silvestrini. **Idee Farbe**.
Baumann & Stromer Verlag, 1994

Norbert Welsch + Claus Chr. Liebmann. **Farben**.
Spektrum Akademischer Verlag, 2003

Robert Somerville. **Fazination Menschlicher Körper**.
Timelife, 1993

Arthur Zajonc. **Die gemeinsame Geschichte von Licht und Bewußtsein**. Rowohlt, 1997

Petra Kellner + Hans Nick Roericht. **Farbe als…**
Lehrmaterial UdK Berlin, 1983

Josef Albers. **Interaction of Color**.
Yale University, 1963

Narciso Silvestrini + Ernst Peter Fischer. **Farbsysteme in Kunst und Wissenschaft**. Dumont Verlag, 2002

Johann Wolfgang von Goethe. **Die Tafeln zur Farbenlehre und deren Erklärungen**. Insel, 1994

Harald Küppers. **Farbe 4. Auflage**.
Callway Verlag, 1987

Johannes Itten. **Kunst der Farbe**.
Seemann Verlag, 2001

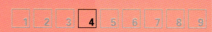

Penguin Books Ltd. **Inside the Personal Computer: A Pop-up Guide**.

Foley, van Dam, Feiner + Hughes. **Computer Graphics, Principles and Practice**. Addison-Wesley, 1990

Chr. Strothotte + Th. Strothotte. **Seeing between the pixels**. Springer

Marc D. Miller + Randy Zaucha. **Color Mac**.
Wolfram's Verlag, 1992

Molly E. Holzschlag. **Farbe für Websites**. Rowohlt, 2002

David Macaulay. **The New Way Things Work**.
Dorling Kindersley Ltd., 1988

Hans Herbert Schulze. **Lexikon Computerwissen**.
Rowohlt, 2002

ADAC. **Faszination Natur und Technik**.
Bertelsmann Verlag, 1996

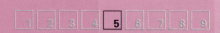

April Greiman. **Hybrid Imagery**.
Architecture Design and Technology Press, 1990

Matthias Nyman. **4 Farben 1 Bild**. Springer, 1998

Rob Carter. **Working with Computer Type 3/color & type**. RotoVision, 1997

Rob Carter. **Working with Computer Type**.
RotoVision, 1996

Ettore Sottsass. **Farbbetrachtungen**.
Abet Laminati, 1993

Nick Clark. **Duotones, Tritones and Quadtones**.
Chronicle Books, 1997

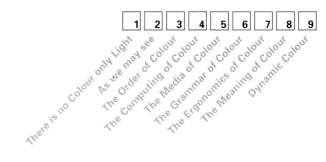

Pina Lewandowsky + Francis Zeischegg. **Visuelles Gestalten mit dem Computer.** Rowohlt, 2002

Veruschka Götz. **Schrift & Farbe am Bildschirm.** Verlag Herman Schmidt, 1997

Veruschka Götz. **Grids for the Internet and other Digital Media.** AVA Publishing SA, 2002

Moritz Zwimpfer. **Farben ordnen, mit Farben spielen.** Verlag Niggli AG, CH, 1997

Shigenobu Kobayashi. **A Book of Colors.** Kodansha International, 1984

Ben Shneiderman. **User Interface Design.** mitp Verlag, 2002

Willberg + Forssman. **Lesetypographie.** Hermann Schmidt Verlag, 1997

Wildbur + Burke. **Information Graphics.** Hermann Schmidt Verlag, 1998

Paul Kahn + Krzysztof Lenk. **Websites visualisieren.** Rowohlt, 2001

Roy Mckelvey. **Hypergraphics.** Rowohlt, 1998

Richard Saul Wurman. **Information anxiety 2.** Que, 2001

Richard Saul Wurman. **Understanding USA.** Ted conferences, 1999

Studio 7.5. **Navigation for the Internet and other Digital Media.** AVA Publishing SA, 2002

Eva Heller. **Wie Farben wirken.** Rowohlt, 1989

Günter Beer. **WebDesign Index 2.** Pepin Press, 2001/2002

Shigenobu Kobayashi. **Color Image Scale.** Kodansha Ltd., 1990

Shigenobu Kobayashi. **Colorist.** Kodansha Ltd., 1998

James Stockton. **Designer's Guide to Color.** Chronicle Books, SF 1984

Ikuyoshi Shibuwaka + Yumi Takahashi. **Designer's Guide to Color 4.** Chronicle Books, SF 1990

**View on Colour.** United Publishers S.A.

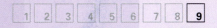

Yugo Nakamura. **New Masters of Flash.** friends of ED, 2000

**Index**

| 1 | 2 | 3 | 4 | 5 | 6 | 7 | 8 | 9 |

1 There is no Colour only Light
2 As we may see
3 The Order of Colour
4 The Computing of Colour
5 The Media of Colour
6 The Grammar of Colour
7 The Ergonomics of Colour
8 The Meaning of Colour
9 Dynamic Colour

| 1 | 2 | 3 | 4 | 5 | 6 | 7 | 8 | 9 |

There is no Colour only Light · As we may see · The Order of Colour · The Computing of Colour · The Media of Colour · The Grammar of Colour · The Ergonomics of Colour · The Meaning of Colour · Dynamic Colour

**Acknowledgements:**

**Brian Morris:** for his patience with us and his trust in us.

**Veruschka Götz:** for being our sister in crime.

**Laura Owen:** for prodding us constantly.

**Hans Nick Roericht, Petra Kellner, Gisela Kasten:** for opening their vaults.

**Christine Strothotte:** for crunching colour by numbers and for strengthening our quest to go beyond science.

**Susanne Stage:** for stamina, persistence and sharing our passion throughout the project.

**Kerstin Kühl:** for her commitment and her willingness to live the same crazy life as we do for the last nine months.

**Studio 7.5:** thanks to the whole crew for support and inspiration.

Carola Zwick and Burkhard Schmitz

May 2003